THE PATH OF LIFE

THE PATH OF LIFE

Benedictine Spirituality for Monks & Lay People

CYPRIAN SMITH OSB

Ampleforth Abbey Press
(Distributed by Gracewing)

AMPLEFORTH ABBEY PRESS
AMPLEFORTH ABBEY
YORK
from
Gracewing
Fowler Wright Books
Southern Avenue, Leominster
Herefordshire HR6 0QF

Printed at the Cromwell Press
Typeset at Ampleforth Abbey
in Monotype Bembo

ISBN 0 85244 302 1

CONTENTS

INTRODUCTION

MANY PEOPLE TODAY are increasingly interested in the life of the Benedictine monk. Often they look at it with a certain envy and nostalgia, sensing that there is something there of incomparable value which they cannot share in completely – perhaps not at all. Are they right to feel this? What are the fundamental aims of Benedictine monastic life? What spiritual resources does it contain? How far can people who are not monks tap into these resources and pursue these aims?

The present book attempts an answer to these questions. My own conviction concerning the aims of a Benedictine monk is that they are not fundamentally different from those of the ordinary Christian. As for the spiritual resources of monastic life, some of these are fully available to the non-monk, others less so. How far they are available and in what way they can be used, it is the aim of this book to show. Not all people can be monks; it is neither necessary nor desirable that they should be. Those who do not have this particular vocation should not therefore feel deprived; their own way of life will contain its own strengths and resources which the monk cannot share in.

The following chapters are all based upon my conferences delivered originally to the novices and juniors of Ampleforth Abbey. They therefore deal with central themes of monastic life and spirituality. I have, however, adapted them and widened their scope so that they may also be relevant to people outside the cloister. If both monks and non-monks can read them with pleasure and profit, my aim will have been realised. My hope and prayer is that this may be so.

CHAPTER 1

LISTENING

THE RULE OF ST BENEDICT opens with the word *ausculta* – listen. Properly understood, this is the key to his whole spiritual teaching. A monk should be above all a listener. So indeed should every Christian. One of the primary purposes of a monastic novitiate is to provide conditions in which we can concentrate on learning the art, realising, of course, that our practice of it will continue throughout life and deepen with age.

But who, or what, are we to listen to? The Rule says: 'to the precepts of the master'. And who is the master? Is it St Benedict himself, perhaps, or our own abbot? In a secondary sense we can certainly say that these are the masters we have to listen to; but our primary and ultimate master is God. The whole spiritual life of the Christian, and especially of the monk, is a process of listening to God, 'inclining the ear of the heart', as the Rule says. This image of the inward ear, the ear of the heart, shows us that our listening is not merely an intellectual or rational activity; it is intuitive, springing from the very core of our being, where we are most open to God, most receptive to the word he speaks. We have to be very quiet and still within ourselves, very alert and attentive, if that word is to resonate properly in our innermost depths, so that we are fully illumined and nourished by it.

We have begun the Christian journey, we have set out upon the monastic path, so as to be taught by God. That is why St Benedict calls the monastery a 'school'. It is not a club for people who have already achieved spiritual perfection; it is a school where people come to learn; and none of us are going to learn anything unless we are prepared to listen.

This idea is not an invention of St Benedict's. It came to him out of the heart of the Jewish and Christian tradition. 'Hear, O Israel' says God to the Chosen People when he is giving them the Law; and Jesus, when telling the parables, cried out: 'Listen, you who have ears to hear!' Jesus himself was the greatest of all listeners; everything he said and did was in response to what he had heard from his Father. This is a fact which is often unnoticed when studying Jesus's life. We think first and foremost of Jesus as the great speaker, the Lion of Judah whose roar inspires terror, whose word shakes the earth, whose command tames the elements, drives out evil spirits and heals the sick. What we overlook is that all this awesome power of Jesus has its origins in silence. In St Luke's Gospel especially, we learn of the long periods of solitary prayer which Jesus spent on hilltops, often during the hours of darkness. What did this prayer consist of? Since he told his disciples not to pour out a torrent of words when praying, we can be sure he took his own advice and avoided talking more than he had to. So his prayer consisted mainly of listening, silent, relaxed, and attentive.

> The Lord has given me
> the tongue of those who are taught,
> that I may know how to sustain with a word
> him that is weary.
>
> Morning by morning he wakens,
> he wakens my ear
> to hear as those who are taught.

2

> The Lord God has opened my ear,
> and I was not rebellious...
> *Isaiah 50:4-5*

These mysterious, prophetic words, spoken by the Suffering Servant in the Book of Isaiah, surely give us the clue to the inner life of Jesus, and indeed of his whole life, showing that it was grounded upon listening. Jesus's obedience to the Father meant that his ear was totally and continually open to the Father's promptings, communicated to him by the Spirit in the depths of his heart. He listened in silence while his Father disclosed his plan and issued his command. This is why Jesus's words and deeds had such tremendous power; they were not his own but came from the one who had sent him; he said nothing to his disciples which he had not previously heard from his Father.

In this he is our exemplar and model. What he did is what we have to do. Furthermore, since we have to do it, we can be sure of being actually able to do it. That is something which always takes us by surprise and slightly dismays us when we are faced with it. We tend to think of Jesus as a sublime but also rather remote figure whose thoughts, deeds and feelings can have very little to do with our own drab and prosaic lives. But that is very far from the truth. We received the Spirit of Jesus at our baptism; his life is now our life; his wisdom and power are ours to draw on. At the Last Supper he went so far as to say that there is nothing he did which we also will not be able to do (*John 14:12*). Why not take that seriously? Why not see for ourselves what happens when we try to do what he did, thinking, speaking and acting in him? A risky venture, certainly; but if we try it we shall never again find our lives boring or meaningless.

So let us assume that we are going to make a serious attempt at this, and base our lives upon listening, as Jesus did. What does this listening consist of; how do we actually set about it? Above all, when and where and how does God speak to us, so that we can know when we should be listening?

The truth of the matter is that God is speaking to us all the time in all the circumstances of life. Every work that we undertake, every experience we undergo, every encounter and relationship we are involved in is a manifestation of God; he is revealing something of himself, speaking something out of his own depths, in all of them.

Our part is to be perpetually alert and attentive, so as to hear and digest what is being said, to catch the flashes of light as the veil is momentarily lifted. However, to do this continually, throughout our waking lives, is extremely difficult. Our tendency to be simply engulfed in everyday affairs, engrossed in them to the point of forgetting God altogether, is far too strong for us at the beginning, when we are just starting out on serious spiritual life. A foundation has to be laid first, which we can then extend and build upon. In other words, we have to start by recognising that there are certain privileged circumstances in which God speaks especially clearly: more clearly than at other times. If we develop the habit of listening in these circumstances, then there is the chance that we may learn later to do it at other times, when God's voice is not so easy to hear, but nevertheless can be heard quite clearly enough once the listening disposition has become habitual and deeply rooted in us. What are these special circumstances, and how should we set about listening in them?

There are two situations, above all, when God speaks to us with particular clarity and force. The first is when we give ourselves to prayer. The second is when we read the Scriptures, or have them read to us, or hear them expounded for us by a preacher (skilled or otherwise). I have not listed these two situations in order of importance; indeed I would find it very difficult to do so, or to discover grounds on which such a judgement could be made. What I am sure of, from my own experience and reading of the Rule of St Benedict, is that they are interrelated and complementary. They feed each other; to listen in the one situation helps us to listen in the other as well.

Prayer and the reading of Scripture are the two main sources for the spiritual life of a Benedictine monk, as they should surely be also for the ordinary Christian living in the world. They are both large topics, and each will need special treatment later on in this book. All I want to point out at the moment is that they are both occasions in which God speaks more clearly than he usually does at other times, and that therefore it is in these above all that we need to develop the habit of listening.

How, then, do we listen during times of prayer? Is there such a thing as a prayer of listening, and if so, what is it like? This is quite a serious question because most of us do not normally consider prayer as being a matter of listening but rather of our talking to God. We are much more concerned with trying to say something to God than with trying to catch what he may be saying to us. Eli's advice to the boy Samuel was that when God called him he should reply, 'Speak, Lord, for your servant is listening.' We prefer to invert that and say instead: 'Listen Lord, for your servant is speaking.' Nevertheless the course counselled by Eli is the wiser one and we ought to follow it. Attempting to follow it takes us into very deep waters indeed, leading us to perceive important truths about the nature of prayer.

Is it not inevitable that when we engage in prayer we should be active, talkers rather than listeners? In the presence of God we unburden ourselves, telling him of our deepest fears, hopes, aspirations, joys, and sorrows, giving thanks, pouring forth praise, requesting help and guidance, not only for ourselves but for others also and for the whole world. We do this both in our private prayer and in the communal prayer of the Church, and there is nothing at all wrong with it. We have even been told clearly by God himself to pray in this way. 'Pour out your hearts before him' says the psalm; and the Lord's prayer is a splendid and concise illustration of how to do it. In all of this we are fairly active, and we are indeed talking rather than listening; it is a very necessary thing for us to do, and it is an important part of prayer.

But it would be a great mistake if we allowed ourselves to think that prayer must always be of this kind, in which we say everything and God says nothing. The Psalmist also says: 'I will listen to what the Lord God says to me.' At times we have to stop talking and be silent, listening with a disciple's ear. This could well be what Jesus really meant when he told his disciples not to use too many words, not to babble on like the pagans. He was not here condemning the practice of repeating words and phrases, which can have a calming and steadying effect upon the mind, and has therefore always been a standard liturgical and devotional practice, in his own day just as in ours. What he was concerned about was not whether we repeat words or not; rather he was reminding us that we also need to learn to pray a different kind of prayer, one in which we are more ready to listen than to speak. Such a prayer comes naturally to anyone who has any sense at all of the transcendence, the otherness, the impenetrable mystery and majesty of God. Hence Ecclesiastes says:

'Be not rash with your mouth, nor let your heart be hasty to utter a word before God, for God is in heaven, and you upon earth; therefore let your words be few.'   *Ecclesiastes 5:2*

This is also the reason for rules of silence in monasteries, and why also in lay life we should try to find or create intervals of silence amid the noise and turmoil of everyday affairs. These silent periods are not meant to be merely mortifying or irritating. Their purpose is to create a climate in which God can speak and be heard. A noisy environment and lifestyle tends to shut God out. As with Elijah on the mountainside, we have to be very still and quiet within ourselves, if we wish to hear God speaking.

Therefore our prayer – especially, perhaps, our private prayer – should contain intervals in which we do not say anything or express any thought or feeling in words, but simply remain still and silent in the presence of God, open and receptive like a flower turning towards the light. It would be very foolish for me or anyone else to attempt to lay down rules about how long or frequent these intervals should be. We can leave this to the inward prompting of the Holy Spirit, who makes them longer or shorter, many or few, depending upon the person or the circumstances. For some people they may be short and few. For others, on the other hand, prayer may consist almost entirely of such silent listening, and speech may be only occasional or sporadic. We need not worry about which path we ought to take here, but simply let ourselves be led easily and naturally, guided by the Holy Spirit without any forcing or strain. Prayer should be refreshment, not hard labour. What matters is not whether our periods of listening are long or short, many or few: what matters is that they exist. They have to exist because prayer is a dialogue with God, not a monologue by us; God's part is more important than ours; what he says to us has far more value than anything we can say to him; and we shall never be able to hear what he says unless we are prepared, at least occasionally, to be silent and listen.

If we do listen then God will certainly speak and we shall be able to hear. Like the boy Samuel, we shall eventually realise who is speaking, and say: 'Speak, Lord, for your servant is listening.' But how does God speak, and how do we recognise his voice? We may not necessarily hear any actual words, or see any visions, although there are undoubtedly people who do. Whether we do or not is not a matter of great importance; it is a simple matter of temperament. There are people who are natural visionaries, whose imagination and sensibility lead them, when stirred by the Spirit of God, to see and hear things. This, I suspect, is a phenomenon which was more common in the past than it is in the present, and if it happens today it is more likely to occur in peasant or rural societies than in the highly literate and mechanised society in which most modern people live, which tends to dull or neutralise our potential for certain kinds of awareness.

No matter; God always finds some way of speaking in the depths of the heart. Often during prayer we shall hear or see nothing at all. We may have a general sense of God' presence, but not of anything specific being communicated. At times even the sense of God's presence may be absent, and we may feel that we have dropped into a dark void. However this may be, there is no need to worry, for God often communicates at the unconscious level, beyond words or images, so that at the time we are not aware of what is happening and it seems to us that nothing is going on at all during the prayer itself. It is often only when we emerge from prayer that we realise that something has happened: suddenly we see an urgent problem in a different light or from a different standpoint, so that we are now able to cope with it; or we find ourselves able to relate to another person more positively and fruitfully than we could before; or we may become aware of some unhealthy attachment which we need to let go of. All of this is a common way in which God speaks and we listen; for many people today the best or even the only one.

The important thing is to be still, silent and receptive – also patient, for what God has spoken in the core of the heart often takes quite a long time to filter through into conscious awareness. In this, as in all spiritual matters, we have to learn how to wait. An oak-tree does not grow from an acorn in a single day, and the Word of God, too, grows slowly and steadily; we shall never be nourished or illuminated by it so long as we are in too much of a hurry.

There is another situation in which God speaks to us clearly, which is the meditative reading of Holy Scripture, called in the traditional monastic language *lectio divina*. Like prayer, this is a spiritual art which takes time to acquire and is not mastered in a single day. Learning how to do it forms a large part of a novice's training in a Benedictine monastery; but it should not be regarded as a practice suitable only for monks.

St Jerome said that ignorance of the Scriptures is ignorance of Christ, and that is something which none of us can afford, whether we are monks or not.

This is not the time or the place for a detailed exposition of *lectio*, its nature and practice. That will have to be left until later. However, a few general remarks can be made here, concentrating on the question of how *lectio* is a form of listening.

First of all we need to realise that when we settle down to read Scripture, we are doing something very different from what we do when we read any other sort of book. Normally when we take up a book, we are looking either for information or for entertainment; if we are fairly sophisticated readers we may also be looking for an experience of beauty, such as we might get from a well-written novel or a fine poem. None of these things, however, is what we are looking for when we read Scripture. Some or all of them may appear from time to time in the biblical books, and hence increase our enjoyment, but they are of secondary, not primary importance. What matters to us is that through the chosen text God is speaking to us; there is a voice whose modulations we are trying to catch; a message we are trying to pick up and digest. The text is not dead but alive; it crackles with the electricity of communication.

That means we have to tune into it, to get onto its wavelength. St Benedict says that before we undertake any good work we should pray for help to complete it; and this is going to be especially true with *lectio* which makes such unusual demands upon us and calls for registers of the mind which we never knew we had. Here again, as in all forms of listening, it is a matter of intuitive perception, of opening the ear of the heart; and that is something we cannot do by relying upon our natural powers alone. God speaks to us through the Spirit, and it is only through the Spirit that we can hear and understand him. Therefore, before starting our *lectio,* it is important to make some prayer to the Holy Spirit asking him for illumination and guidance. Then, after pausing for a few moments of silence, placing ourselves in the presence of God, we can begin our reading.

The reading itself should be slow and meditative, with frequent pauses, so as to let the words resonate in the mind, and to allow ourselves to ponder on them and extract their meaning. This is not an occasion for 'fast reading' techniques, which would undermine the whole purpose of what we are about. Spiritual food, like physical food, cannot be 'bolted' if we want to be properly nourished by it. We should regard what we read as being addressed to us personally, in the very situation which we find ourselves in at the moment. Its relevance to ourselves, however, may not be immediately apparent, and we need to give it time and patience in order to let it unfold. Hence the frequent pauses for reflection and prayer. Even so there may be many resonances in the text which we are not aware of straight away; as with prayer, it is often not until the operation is actually over that certain aspects of the message become clear. For this reason I have found it fruitful to do lectio as early in the day as possible so that my mind can revert to it from time to time as the day progresses, sounding new depths and perceiving further applications which could not be seen at first.

A question now arises as to what is meant by this word 'message'. If the Scripture we read is to be seen as a message addressed to us, then are we not regarding lectio as a form of divination, seeking supernatural guidance from it in the same way as people in the ancient pagan world sought messages from the gods by observing the flight of birds, by manipulating divination sticks, or by pulling out the entrails of animals?

In a sense, yes we are; the Scriptural text is truly an oracle which will show us the spiritual meaning of the situation we are in, and help us to discern what sort of conduct is appropriate for it. We shall investigate this aspect of *lectio* further in the chapter dedicated to it. But for the moment we should realise that reading Scripture is not exactly like reading Tarot cards or consulting the I-Ching. In those non-Christian forms of divination all we are looking for is an answer to the problem perplexing us; the question of who it is who is speaking or providing the answer matters very little, provided we believe what we are told and act upon it. But lectio does not merely answer our questions or help us solve our problems. It puts us in touch with God, it establishes a relationship with him, just as prayer does and also as the sacraments of the Church do in a slightly different way. It is a meeting-point, a place of encounter; and the more we resort to it the more our relationship with God will deepen. This relationship, and its ever-increasing depth, is the true purpose of lectio. It does not merely give us guidance for conduct; it also reveals something about God, about ourselves and where we stand with him. The question of who is speaking is of paramount importance for us. Indeed the message, if we are going to call it that, derives its whole value from the fact that it is from God and that it is building up our relationship with him.

That is probably why from Old Testament times until today, Jews and Christians have been discouraged from practising pagan forms of divination. It is not necessarily that these forms are evil, though some of them may be, especially when we are not at all sure who or what is speaking through them. It is more that for us such practices are unnecessary and also imply a kind of infidelity. Why ask questions of stars or yarrow-stalks when we have God speaking to us in person, in ways which not only give us guidance but also build up that relationship with him which is the true goal of our existence? When we have his word to feed on, to look for supplementary sources of nourishment would be both foolish and ungrateful.

There is quite a lot more to be said about *lectio,* but for the moment we can leave it. The important thing to do now is to see it as a form of listening, of opening the ear of the heart, in an attitude of quiet confidence, docility, and receptivity. If we do this in *lectio* we shall find it easier to do in prayer as well; and if we do it in prayer we shall find it easier to do in *lectio.* Both are modes of listening, and they feed each other. They put us into communication with God, establishing and deepening our proper relationship with him.

As we learn progressively to hear and respond to the word of God in these privileged circumstances, we can also learn to do the same in all the circumstances of our daily lives, even the most humdrum, the most uncongenial, the most apparently profane. The disciple's ear, open and attentive, can hear God speaking in the bus-queue, in the supermarket, in the conversation of a tiresomely boring or demanding person, and know instinctively how to respond. That is the supreme spiritual art. Haven't you learned it yet? Of course you haven't. It takes a

13

LISTENING

lifetime to learn it, and once you have perfected it there will be no reason for you to continue your life on this earth, for you will have fulfilled the purpose of your existence. But if you want to get there, you have to start now.

CHAPTER 2

STABILITY

FOR MANY PEOPLE living in the world monastic life seems profoundly mysterious and impenetrable. Perhaps this will always be so; certainly it seems to have always been so. It is not merely the external trappings of monasticism that create the problem: black robes, hoods, gothic arches and tinkling bells. Rather it is the deeper question of what the monk's life is all about. Why do people choose to live in this peculiar way? What value do they see in it; what good is it going to do, either for themselves or for anyone else?

It is not easy to give a short, clear answer to this question. There is much in monastic life that cannot be conveyed by words; we can only come to understand it by living it, by experiencing it from the inside. But if there is anything at all that expresses the essence of our ideal, clearly and briefly, it is surely the three vows which we take when we commit ourselves definitively to the monastery. These point unmistakably to our ultimate aim, to our final hope; also to the means by which we seek to achieve our end. If, then, we understand these vows we shall have grasped the essence of monastic life; we shall know, at least in outline, what it is all about.

The three vows are: stability, *conversatio morum*, and obedience. It will be worth our while to examine each of these in turn. This will not only be profitable to monks, by reminding them of what they have pledged themselves to; it will be helpful also to people outside the monastery, who can then ask themselves how far the values expressed in these vows are relevant to them, and how far they can live them out in the circumstances of their own lives. My own conviction is that all three of them are relevant, and that if they are properly understood, ways can be found of realising them in almost any walk of life whatever.

The vow which at first sight seems most resistant to this kind of wider application is the first, the vow of stability. After all, is this not the specifically monastic vow which distinguishes monastic life most sharply from other forms of religious life? Friars, Jesuits, missionaries, secular priests do not take this vow, since it contradicts that freedom of movement which is an intrinsic part of their own vocation. For what does a monk promise when he takes this vow? He promises that henceforth his life will be rooted within the monastery. He will live and work within the area defined as 'monastic enclosure'; he will not leave that area except in cases of necessity, and even then only with the permission of his superior. Nothing could be more remote than this from the normal lifestyle of people who are not monks. How, then, could the vow of stability have any relevance for them? Why, indeed, do the monks themselves take it, thereby cutting themselves off from much that is normal and natural in human life?

'The letter kills, the spirit gives life.' This is a basic principle of Scriptural interpretation. By it we understand that in a Scriptural text there are two levels of meaning: there is the literal, obvious meaning, and there is the deeper, underlying meaning. The advantage with the literal meaning is that it is usually simple and easy to grasp, and we can do that by means of our natural human power of reason. Unfortunately this literal meaning also has a disadvantage, which is that it is often rather limited, even trivial, and not very relevant to people like ourselves, living in an epoch and cultural milieu very different from that of the biblical authors.

With the deeper, underlying meaning the situation is the exact opposite. It is almost impossible to grasp this by means of natural human reasoning; an intuitive flair is needed, aided by the Holy Spirit. That is the problem with it. Its advantage, on the other hand, is that if we succeed in grasping it we shall find it fully and deeply relevant to ourselves and to the circumstances we find ourselves in. It has a universality and depth which the literal meaning often lacks. It is, in fact, the true meaning, because it is transforming and life-giving; it makes the text come alive, which when understood only on the literal level remains dead.

The same principle applies to the three monastic vows. They, too, have a letter and a spirit, an outward literal observance and an inward spiritual meaning. It is the latter which truly matters; without it monastic life is only an empty shell. A monk might appear to be observing the vow of stability, for example, in a manner which is perfect and above reproach; while inwardly, in his heart, he is a thousand miles away from it. We must therefore distinguish clearly between what is outward in this vow and what is inward. Needless to say, it is the inward meaning alone which has relevance to people who are not monks.

The outward observance of stability is, as we have already seen, the monk's physical and geographical rootedness in the monastery, and his obligation to remain within the defined area of enclosure. What, then, is the inward dimension? It is a certain attitude of mind, a certain disposition of the heart. We train ourselves to become, with the help of the Holy Spirit, inwardly stable as well.

What does this mean, to be inwardly stable? In the Scriptures, especially, perhaps, in the Old Testament, there is much talk of a certain quality of God which in Hebrew is called *hesed*. The word has been translated in a variety of ways, but perhaps the best rendering in English is 'steadfast love.' It is God's *hesed*, his steadfast love, which makes him thoroughly reliable, constant and faithful. God is not fickle, changeable or wayward in his relationship with us. His desire is to draw us all into joy and fulfilment through union with him, and this desire of his is utterly constant and unwavering. Even our infidelity and ingratitude do not put him off. In Psalm 88 he says of David:

'My steadfast love I will keep for him forever,
and my covenant will stand firm for him...

If his children forsake my law
and do not walk according to my ordinances...

Then I will punish their transgressions with the rod
and their iniquity with scourges;
but I will not remove from him my steadfast love,
or be false to my faithfulness.'
Psalm 88: 28, 30, 32-33

God is utterly resolved on the sanctification and glorification of the human race; he is not going to rest until that purpose has been achieved; nothing is going to shake him from that resolve. This unwavering determination, this total reliability of God is often described in Scripture by the image of the rock. 'Blessed be my rock!' cries the Psalmist (*Psalm 17:46*) and Jesus applies the same image to himself and his own message,

18

saying that his words are a rock, a stable foundation for us to build our lives upon. What all this means is that God's *hesed,* his unchanging determination to bring us to glory, creates for us an axis, a firm unchanging centre in a shifting, fluctuating world. Whoever finds that centre, whoever puts down roots in it, will never be shaken or swept away by the changing tides of fortune.

This is what God is like; he is utterly reliable and stable. If we look honestly, however, at ourselves and at our own lives, we have to admit sadly that they are very different. We are terribly changeable and wayward; terribly fickle. The slightest influence upon us – the weather, perhaps, or something we have eaten – is enough to change our mood and throw us off course. This makes it extremely difficult for us to commit ourselves permanently to anyone or anything. Nothing frightens us more than the prospect of having to hold to a particular course, come what may. This deep instability in our nature corrodes our marriages, our religious vocations, our friendships, our work. We are prey to our passing moods: sometimes cheerful, sometimes depressed, sometimes kind and tolerant, sometimes hard and impatient. Environmental circumstances, and the company we keep – all of these affect the way we feel and behave. At times we have reason to wonder whether we possess such a thing as a single, unified personality. We are one sort of person at home, and quite a different one at work; another person in the morning and yet another in the evening. To make things worse we are living in a world and a culture which are undergoing chaotic and frenetic change: in customs, attitudes, social and political insti-tutions. Stability is not exactly the word which springs most

19

immediately to mind when we try to describe ourselves or our world.

To remedy this situation is one of the primary aims of monastic life, as it is of all Christian life. But how do we effect this remedy? We do it by rooting ourselves in God, by making God the real centre of our lives. If God is the real, and not merely theoretical, axis around which our lives revolve,then he imparts to us over the years some of his own qualities, including his *hesed,* his steadfast love, his stability. The stability of God finds its analogue and reflection in us. We hail God as 'the Rock'; and every Christian, perhaps especially the monk, becomes something of a rock as well – steady, unshakeable; a firm centre in a shifting and transient world.

This is the true stability of the heart, the inner meaning and purpose of the vow. Few people will be able to deny that it is a goal worth striving for, whether they are monks or not. Most of us hanker after it, consciously or unconsciously. It is gained by rooting ourselves in God. But how can we do that? It sounds as though we are merely replacing one problem with another, offering an answer which is not an answer but merely a still more impenetrable mystery.

If we look at some of the ways in which the monk tries to fulfil his vow, we shall get some inkling of how stability of the heart can be attained.

In attempting to be faithful to his vow, the monk gradually learns, with prayer and with the grace of God, to gain some measure of detachment from his passing moods. He is obliged to live with the same people, in the same place, to do the same work, to go through the same liturgical routine, day after day, month after month, year after year. There are bound to be times when this gets very stale and monotonous. That is to be expected. Sometimes the life is satisfying and rewarding, but we cannot count on it always being so. Whatever the monk's feeling may be about what he has been given, however, he sticks to it. He perseveres in the daily hours of communal prayer, whether he enjoys them or not. He is faithful to his work and his commitment to the the service of the brethren, despite his passing feelings.

After a while he becomes aware of two quite distinct levels in his mind and heart, levels which exist simultaneously. On the one hand, there are the daily ups and downs, with their concomitant fluctuations of mood. On the other hand, there is an abiding sense that however things may be going, even though they may not seem at the moment to be going particularly well, he is nevertheless in the right place, doing the right thing with the right people. The passing moods cease to matter; they are recognised as transient and ephemeral, like clouds in the sky. Gradually he becomes aware of a still centre in the heart which is not subject to mood-swings or external conditioning. Many names have been given to this centre: Jerusalem; the Ground of the Soul; the Interior Castle; the Citadel; the Bride. Once we have become aware of it, and begun to ground ourselves upon it, we have started to achieve inner stability.

This awareness will not dawn, however, unless we create the conditions for it, and this is done in two ways. The first is to stay put and not run away from the situation we are in, whatever our present feelings about it may be. The second is to pray, and above all to pray in a certain way. The way in question consists of an act of surrender, of acceptance of the Will of God as manifested in the present moment and the present circumstances. We relax into those circumstances, we go loose, we let go of worry, and trust in God who is leading us and carrying us. Doing this in prayer helps us to do it in our other occupations as well; it melts the heart, making it docile and receptive, so that it can respond to the promptings of the Spirit and be strengthened by them to overcome our innate stubbornness and selfishness.

It is not surprising that as we try to understand the vow and practice of stability we find prayer at the heart of it. Prayer is at the heart of everything in the spiritual life, and nothing can be understood or achieved apart from it. This is not the place, however, for a detailed discussion of prayer; that will have to come later. For the moment we can conclude with a few simple and practical remarks on the practice of stability and how to develop it.

First, a moment's reflection should suffice for us to see that in its inner spiritual essence it is not by any means exclusively a monastic virtue but it can be practised in many different walks of life. Certainly the monk has an enormous advantage, strengthened as he is by his vow, by his general lifestyle, and by the means of grace daily available to him: communal and private prayer, the sacraments and spiritual reading.

But many people in the world, are often forced to develop a stable heart, simply in order to cope with the situation they are in. The husband who does overtime in order to earn enough to keep his family; the wife who prepares meals and dresses the children day after day; such people could not carry on unless they had achieved some degree of inner stability. Perhaps women are forced to develop the virtue more often than men, since as mothers and housewives it is less easy for them to run away from the daily drudgery, to find escapes and outlets. However, the stability which people develop in circumstances of this kind is not always the real thing; it can be no more than a makeshift human substitute, a kind of passive, helpless resignation, saying: 'Well, I can't change any of this, so I may as well make the best of it.' This is not true stability because it lacks the fire of the Spirit, which enables us not merely to <u>accept</u> but actually to <u>want</u> the situation given to us because we find God in it. Only through regular prayer and frequent use of the sacraments can we hope to enter the Interior Castle; so these means are as essential for those who are not monks as for those who are.

So, my first practical hint is: do not run away from your present situation or try to change it, unless it is clearly bad and needs to be changed. Obviously there are times when we do need to change. If we are in a monastery, we may find that we are not suited to the life and need to leave. If we are lay people working in the world, we may need to change our job, for a variety of perfectly good reasons: we are not earning enough to support our family, for example, or the work itself may be immoral and corrupting.

But in general, in today's Western world, we are inclined to be too quick to change. We blame circumstances for our unhappiness and restlessness, when the true problem is with ourselves. It is more often we who need to change, rather than the external situation. All the major spiritual teachers of the world have been telling us this for centuries, but we are very reluctant to believe it. We shall make no progress spiritually unless we do believe it, stop running away, and open ourselves up generously to God in the actual situation which is ours at this present moment. The grass is not really greener on the other side of the fence; the kingdom of Heaven is not far away in some impossibly remote place; it is here and now, and we are more likely to find it by staying put in our monastery, in our family, in our present work, than by running off somewhere else.

The second hint is: do not run away from yourself. Accepting the challenge of an uncongenial situation, and remaining within it, naturally stirs up quite a lot of mental and emotional turbulence. At times we shall feel angry or frustrated; certain people will get on our nerves and irritate us almost beyond endurance; there will be occasions when we shall feel we have been unjustly treated, and indeed we may really have been so. This churns us up inside, and brings us face to face with many weaknesses and limitations of our own character. We may do or say things which we regret and which do not show up in a very favourable light. It is remarkably difficult to face us to the less admirable elements in our own character, to admit and accept our faults and weaknesses. Yet to do so is the only way to make any real spiritual progress. We cannot be healed until we recognise that we are sick, we cannot be made strong until we know our own weakness. Knowing it means experiencing it, having our noses rubbed in it. Having it healed means offering it to God.

Here religion complements and perfects the work of the psychiatrist. Psychiatry can confront us with the dark and chaotic elements in the unconscious mind; it can make them conscious, so that we are aware of them. Some psychiatrists give the impression of thinking that this awareness alone brings healing. I doubt very much whether it does. We can be fully aware of violent and destructive passions or fatal weaknesses within ourselves without being able to do anything whatever to overcome them. They are too strong for us; we are dominated and enslaved by them. At this point a spiritual remedy is needed. The priest or spiritual director can remind us that we are still loved by God, still valued, despite our weaknesses and various backslidings. Through sacramental Confession, Holy Communion, and by casting our problems onto God in prayer, we can open ourselves up to the Holy Spirit so that we can be really healed. Healing takes many forms. Sometimes the weakness or passion which is troubling us is actually overcome; sometimes we are enabled simply to live with it, to cope with it, to circumscribe its influence so that it does not do too much harm, either to ourselves or to others. But whatever form healing takes, it will always be given, if we fulfil the two conditions: first, to face and acknowledge the dark areas within ourselves; second, to cast them into the ocean of God's mercy, through prayer and the sacraments.

We are here on the brink of a great mystery, one of the great treasures of our spiritual tradition: the knowledge of what rôle our weaknesses play in our spiritual development, of how they can be made to work for us instead of against us, how they can lead to progress instead of regress. But this is a matter to be investigated more fully later on, when we look at the vow of *conversatio morum* which concerns the mystery of transformation at the heart of Christian life.

What we need to grasp now is that the vow of stability which the monk takes is simply a way of preparing the ground so that the Holy Spirit can act and confer on him the gift of inner stability, which is a quality of the heart, an attitude or disposition of the mind. This attitude or disposition of the mind is an essential feature of all Christian life, and not of monastic life alone. If we are not monks, we are not thereby dispensed from seeking it; it is obviously so necessary. The way to find it lies in acceptance of where we are, acceptance of ourselves, and deep, earnest prayer. That will lead us into the Interior Castle, and ground our lives upon the Rock.

CHAPTER 3

CONVERSATIO MORUM

THIS VOW RETAINS its Latin name because scholars disagree on exactly how to translate it. We are not concerned here with scholarly or academic questions, so there is no need to go into that particular debate. What St Benedict means by the term *conversátio morum* is clear enough from the way he uses it: he is talking about a change of direction in our lives, a pursuit of goals different from those we have pursued hitherto. When a monk takes this vow, he is promising to change his way of life; from now on, both his inner attitude and his outward behaviour are going to be different from what is regarded as normal in the world. This is the letter, or surface meaning of the vow. There is also the spirit, however, which is the inner meaning, present in this as in all the vows. Here we touch upon the mystery of transformation, whereby we do not merely think and behave in a different way from before, but actually become a different person, a different kind of being. One of the greatest treasures of Catholic Christianity is the knowledge that such a radical transformation is really possible. Holiness is not merely imputed to the fully committed Christian, it is imparted by the energising and illuminating Spirit. We are not merely reckoned as holy; we become so – if we truly desire it, and are prepared to pay the price, which is the total surrender of self.

Let us begin, then, by looking at the literal, that is, the surface meaning of the vow, which is a change in our attitude and behaviour. All Christians, and not monks alone, are called to recognise that there is more to life than the pursuit of worldly ends. Most people live as though this world and this

27

life were the only ones we can ever know, and therefore devote themselves to the single-minded pursuit of what this world has to offer: power, pleasure, money, material security, social status... the list is almost endless; but perhaps power, pleasure and money are the principal goals we tend to focus upon. The pursuit of these ends is fuelled by the corresponding passions: pride, sensuality and possessiveness. We need to recognise, however, that it is not the objects of these passions which are bad. There is nothing wrong with exercising power provided we are using it not for ourselves but for the good of others. There is nothing wrong with pleasure, either, in itself; it would be a miserable world indeed if we could never enjoy ourselves with a good conscience. We tend, however, to seek pleasure in ways which harm ourselves and others, and that is where the evil lies. Money, too can be used for good or for ill; in itself it is neutral. Nor is it necessarily a bad thing to have possessions, provided we really need them and use them well.

The problem with these passions is that we cannot control them and they are liable to take us over. When that happens, evil inevitably results. We can no longer relate to other people in a positive and harmonious way; they have become for us mere objects to be manipulated for our own ends. We can no longer relate to God, either, because that involves the surrender of the very self which we are studiously building up by feeding our passions. Alienated from God and from our fellow humans, what satisfaction or fulfilment are we going to find in life? The worldly ends which we are pursuing are not going to fill this gap. Even if we obtain what we are striving for we shall not be happy. To seek ultimate fulfilment in power, pleasure, or money is like drinking salt water; the more we drink, the thirstier we become.

By pledging himself to monastic life in the vow of *conversatio morum*, the monk rejects these three passions and distances himself from them. The thirst for power is negated by obedience and humility; the search for pleasure by celibacy and frugality; the hunger for possessions by communal ownership. There is no room either, in monastic life, for money-grabbing or avarice. Monks do, indeed, work in order to earn their living; but it has to be honest work, and restraints are imposed to prevent it from becoming a money-making racket. St Benedict says that if there are craftsmen in the monastery, they must sell their goods at a rate slightly cheaper than what is normal in the world. That is a precaution to prevent greed or avarice from creeping in; and even in today's world, where the economic conditions are very different from what they were in St Benedict's time, monastic communities take great care not to become commercial exploiters.

Conversatio morum would, however, be a very negative thing if it did no more than mortify the selfish passions. That is only one side of the coin. On the other side something more positive emerges. The energies which cannot express themselves in selfish ways must not be left idle or pent up; some outlet must be found for them, so they are redirected to the service of God and of the brethren, in prayers, reading and constructive work for the good of others. It is very important for monks to work. This not only prevents them from being parasites on society, it also channels basic human drives and spiritualises raw human energies. Work is thus not merely a kind of occupational therapy to fill in the time between the hours of prayer; it has its own special value as an agent for spiritual growth. It is an intrinsic part of *conversatio morum*.

Another element in this vow is that the monk who takes it is opting for life in a community which is content to be on the margin of society, which does not seek fame or celebrity, does not strive to be at the centre of things or exert influence over contemporary affairs, does not want involvement in them. This attitude is called *fuga mundi,* or flight from the world. St Benedict himself does not use the term; but the fact that he endorsed it is clear from almost every page of his Rule. It is one of the paradoxes of human life that monastic communities which shun the limelight nevertheless become famous and well known, and by striving not to exert influence become, in fact, extremely influential. Such influence is not deliberately sought, however, either by the individual monk or by his community; once monks do begin to seek it then it is all over with them. A monastery which becomes large, famous, and wealthy will have problems, which only the most rigorous fidelity to the Gospel can hope to counteract. 'How difficult it is for a rich man to enter the Kingdom of God!' declares Jesus; and we can be rich in many ways, not by any means in money alone.

All that has been said so far helps us to gain some idea of what *conversatio morum* is. Yet we are still hedging, still lingering on the outskirts of the vow; we have not yet given a plain, simple statement of what it is really all about. To do so is, of course, a risky business, but it seems to me that essentially what we are promising in *conversatio* is that from now on God, and not self, will be at the centre of our life. That is easy to promise, very hard to achieve; even impossible to achieve without the grace of God. If I rely on my human powers alone, I cannot help seeing myself as the centre of everything, and other people, and the world around me, as having value and meaning only in relation to me, to my needs and ends. I can try to shift my centre of gravity, and live for God and for others rather than for myself; but I shall never succeed in this unless the Spirit of God enters in, takes charge, and changes me into a new person and a new being. That is the inner and most important aspect of the vow, but before we embark on that, perhaps we ought to ask how much of what has been said so far is relevant to people who are not monks? Is it valid only within the monastic enclosure, or has it a wider application?

To tackle this theme is a highly dangerous enterprise for a monk who has deliberately chosen to live on the margin of society. I do not wish to swell the already bursting ranks of zealous but naïve clergymen, anxious to prove their relevance to society by making hasty public pronouncements on matters they know next to nothing about. People who do not know the world well should beware of making dogmatic assertions or wild generalisations about it. Any remarks I make on this topic should, therefore, be taken for what they are: hints and suggestions, made very tentatively, for people to take or leave as they wish. I cannot set myself up as any kind of prophet or visionary, speaking inspired words out of the heart of his own illumination.

There is one thing, however, which I feel I can affirm with some confidence, and that is that people living in the world must pray, often and deeply. This is the most important single thing that a human being can do, and it is especially urgent in today's world. I am not saying that it is the whole of life, or that we should neglect our other duties and commitments in order to pursue it. Neither am I saying that on its own it will resolve all our problems, as though the world could be saved simply by our sitting comfortably and giving off the appropriate 'vibes' of love and peace. Nevertheless it is central and vital, and all who can do it must do it. It is principally through prayer that human hearts are changed, and unless that happens nothing in the external world is going to change very much either. The more this book unfolds, the more it seems to me that it is essentially about prayer. I make no apology for that. Later on we shall have to look at the matter specifically, as a theme in its own right; for the moment it is enough to note that it is an intrinsic part of *conversatio morum*, and for everyone, not monks alone. Hearts have to be changed, and the grace of God has to be let into the world. Are those two ways of saying the same thing? Not quite. To talk of God's grace entering into the world is to hint at the mystery of cosmic transformation, to suggest that not only our hearts, but the universe as well, are destined to be transformed. This is a mystery as yet only dimly understood; but what is certain is that prayer is right at the heart of it.

A critical moment in the spiritual life of people living in the world is the point at which prayer flows into the area of work and everyday affairs. This junction of the spiritual and the temporal, this intersection of time and eternity, needs very delicate handling, but we have to attempt it. Here again there is much to be said which cannot be discussed now, but which we shall try to develop more fully in a later chapter: *Making Life a Unity*. What can be said here and now is that petitionary prayer plays an important rôle in this linking of the spiritual with the temporal. The Rule of St Benedict tells us that before we undertake any good work we should pray to God to bring it to perfection. That is good advice for anyone, whether in the cloister or out of it. It does not simply mean, however, asking God to make our work a success, in the sense of a job efficiently and effectively done. It also means asking for our motives to be purified, so that what we do is done for God and for other people, not for ourselves.

Having done this, can we then get on with the job with a clear conscience, confident that it is all for the Kingdom? Yes, but there is also a caution. St Benedict says we should pray before undertaking any good work. Works which are not good in themselves cannot be spiritualised, however noble our intention. Here is a difficulty. In order to earn one's living in the world, one finds oneself increasingly caught up in operations of dubious morality. How many politicians, lawyers, doctors, and businessmen can safely close their eyes in sleep, knowing that during the day which has passed, they have not carried out actions which are, to say the least, morally ambiguous? Is it really possible to live in the world and keep one's hands clean at the same time?

It is possible, though not easy, and we should not condemn ourselves too severely if we sometimes fail. We need a firm grasp of basic moral principles, to start with; and this is immensely helped by the practice of *lectio* or spiritual reading which reminds us daily of the Law of God and of the relations which ought to prevail between him and us, between ourselves and other people. With those basic principles firmly rooted in our minds, we can then undertake the delicate task of applying them to the shifting, often bewildering world of practical applications, concrete decisions to be taken in individual circumstances. Sometimes we can take advice from people we trust and respect, but often we have to make snap

THE PATH OF LIFE

decisions on the spur of the moment, and hope that they are the right ones. There may well be many occasions when we wonder whether we have, in fact, done the right thing. We cannot expect certainty at all times. All we can do is to pray for purity of motive, and then act, according to whatever lights we have, entrusting the outcome to God.

It is good to doubt oneself and one's own motives. There is something very frightening about people who are always convinced of their own rightness; they are probably fooling themselves and not seeing the unflattering truth. Much of the worst harm is done in the world by people of this kind, who inflict terrible suffering on others without any pang of regret, basking meanwhile in the warmth of what they think is their own virtue. Our motives are often suspect: 'Cleanse me of my secret faults' prays the Psalmist. At the same time we must not let self-doubt paralyse us, so that we become incapable of action. If we regularly ponder on the law of God, recognise our own weaknesses and pray for help, then we ought to be able to act with a clear conscience, offering all to God for the furthering of his Kingdom.

Another important principle to remember when living in the world is not to be afraid to stand up and be counted. Christianity today is a minority religion – perhaps it has always been so. The fully believing and practising Christian will often be at variance with the prevailing thought and behaviour of contemporary society. It is not easy to believe in God in modern Europe or America, where only scientific knowledge is regarded as true, where religious perception is regarded as mere subjective feeling, where the very notion of 'religious truth' is thought of as a contradiction in terms, and where an educational policy obsessed with the acquisition of skills and techniques seems bent on stifling the intuitive faculties which might open the heart to God. To obey God, to tune into his Will, is not easy either, when all the social pleasures urge us to the opposite, to the pursuit of short-term benefits at least cost to ourselves. How can we live the Christian life in a world where nothing is 'true' or 'false,' 'right' or 'wrong,' but only 'helpful' or 'unhelpful' ? This calls for courage and faith, and the readiness to face unpopularity; but if we do our best we shall be given help, find refreshment at times, and friends in unexpected places. The spirituality of everyday life is an unending topic, and we shall return to various other aspects of it in later chapters; but now we need to look beneath the surface of the vow we are considering, and try to grasp something of its deeper, underlying meaning. Here we enter the mystery of transformation, whereby the grace of God turns us into a new being, 'a new creation.'

Certain pioneers of modern psychology, notably CG Jung, have complained that the modern church often fails to heal or change people because it focuses too much on the externals of religion – dogma, cult, morality – and does not touch the depths of the human heart. There is some truth in this accusation. We cannot expect to change if we concentrate on the sort of person we want to be or ought to be. The first step is to recognise or come to terms with the person we actually are. This is not always very pleasant, but it has to be done. What is true of bodily medicine is also true of spiritual medicine. No one can embark on a course of physiotherapy without first having a neurological check-up, so that it can be seen what needs to be done and what can be done. The more we see of who and what we are now, the more we are able to open it all up to the grace of God, so that healing can come about.

Monastic life is remarkably effective at forcing us to recognise the truth about what we really are. The various demands of the life, in terms of prayer and work, combined with the inevitable rubbing against other people by living and working with them, soon confronts us with our weaknesses and limitations. In this respect it resembles family life, and people living in the world can thus share the monk's experience, provided that their family life is genuine – that the members of the family do find time to live and communicate with each other, instead of being dominated and mesmerised by the television. If so far we have managed to remain ignorant of our shortcomings and faults of character, we can be sure of finding helpful people in our monasteries or families who will be only too happy to point them out to us. Many of these less creditable aspects of ourselves will surface spontaneously, without needing anyone else's 'help'!

Sooner or later we are going to be faced with what are called 'negative' emotions: fear, anger, frustration, boredom, hate, lust – the list is endless. For a monk the confrontation with these dark forces comes as something of a shock. Many people when they join monasteries harbour the unconscious notion that the mere fact of living the monastic life ought to make them holy. Negative emotions, they think, ought not to exist in the cloister. If they occur, then something must have gone wrong. Suppose a monk settles down to pray and finds that his mind, instead of contemplating God, is full of rancour or impatience or sexual desire? How is he going to react to this unwelcome experience? Very often it causes him to doubt the genuineness of his vocation. It makes him think that he has not the necessary qualities for living the monastic life; he is not a 'good enough person'.

In fact the reverse is true. The welling up of these dark thoughts shows that the Spirit is truly active, penetrating the depths of the heart, and therefore churning up a certain amount of mud and sediment. If we wait patiently, do not allow ourselves to be discouraged or frightened, and simply commit ourselves to God, the murky water will eventually clear. The experience of Bernadette in the cave at Lourdes is profoundly symbolic. The spring, when she first found it, was muddy and dark and she was reluctant to drink it. Later it became a healing spring for thousands of pilgrims. We all carry within ourselves a cave and a spring, and we must expect the water to be rather cloudy at first before it becomes clear, transparent and refreshing. Sitting it out, staring the darkness in the face, waiting patiently for God to save – this gradually frees us from enslavement to negative emotions and turns us into a different sort of person.

But there is a still deeper level for us to explore if we want to really penetrate the mystery of transformation. Negative emotions are, after all, transient and fleeting. But what of those temperamental weaknesses and shortcomings which are permanently and deeply rooted in our character, and which even prayer and patience seem unable to shift? Many of us have physical weaknesses or ailments which exasperate and humiliate us, and which we are quite powerless to shake off. Many of us, also, have a leaning towards some vice or enslaving habit – a craving for alcohol, for example, or tobacco, or some form of disordered sexual desire. These things seem to alienate us from God, place us in the category of those who do not belong in the Kingdom. Yet almost all people, perhaps everywhere, even the strongest, have some-where within them an area of weakness which undermines them just when they think they are going to achieve something worthwhile.

Ancient myths and legends often present us with the tragic figure of the hero, who is strong in most ways but who has some fatal area of vulnerability which eventually brings about his downfall. The story of Achilles springs most readily to mind – Achilles who could not be overthrown unless he was wounded in his heel. Even more suggestive is the legend of Siegfried, who after he had slain the dragon, washed himself in its blood, so that its power flowed into him. But while he was doing this, a leaf fell from an overhanging tree and brushed him between the shoulders. From then on he could not be wounded in any part of his body – except for the place where he had been touched by the leaf.

There is much wisdom in these ancient tales, with their picture of human nature as essentially good but fatally flawed. Christianity, however, has deepened the picture by adding a new dimension. It is only on the purely natural and human level that these areas of weakness in us are fatal. On the spiritual level they can become sources of strength, working for us instead of against us. They can become means of progress – if we take them and use them in the right way.

The classic case of this is St Paul. It is well known that he suffered from some kind of weakness or ailment which he refers to as 'an angel from Satan' which buffeted him, causing him acute humiliation and discouragement. There has been much speculation on what exactly this affliction was. Some have imagined it to be a physical malady such as epilepsy – an illness often interpreted in the ancient world as possession by a god. Others have thought it some psychological neurosis, or some form of disordered sexual desire. Whatever it was, it was clearly a very heavy burden for him, so that he prayed God three times to take it away, to which he received this extraordinary reply:

> 'My grace is sufficient for you, for my power is made perfect in weakness.'   *2 Cor 12:9*

Paul was a strong-willed man, naturally inclined to arrogance and furthermore empowered by the Spirit of God. He needed his affliction, his 'angel of Satan', to keep him humble, to stop him becoming proud, and to remind him to depend on God rather than on his own strength. Thus kept in the right relationship with God, he could continue to be God's instrument and progress further and further along the path to union with God. His fatal flaw was, from a certain point of view, his greatest gift.

This gives the writings of Paul their greatest fascination; the fact that he talks from a point of weakness not of strength. His letters do not have the luminous serenity of a Zen or Taoist sage, speaking out of the heart of his own enlightenment. He is struggling in the mud and the mire, like the rest of us. His faults of character are evident enough: the bullying, hectoring tone, the trumpeting of his own achievements, the breathtaking cheek of 'Be imitators of me, as I am of Christ.' But coupled with this we see his extraordinary flashes of vision, his unparalleled depth of understanding of the mystery of Christ which possessed him utterly and to which he gave his entire life, so that he thoroughly deserves the title of saint. That such rough material could be such a powerful instrument for God's purposes shows us what divine grace can achieve, and above all that our weaknesses have an essential and positive rôle in our spiritual progress.

So what are we to do when faced with weaknesses of this kind in ourselves? First, acknowledge them, recognise them, and, above all, call them by their proper name. If, for example, I am greatly shaken by lustful desire, then I should call it that, and not try to disguise it in fine words, saying for example: 'This is a burning and all-consuming passion, which time can never erase and even death will be unable to destroy.' It is simpler and more honest to call it lust, then let go of it, casting it onto the mercy of God. And so we should do with all the other discreditable desires and weaknesses which afflict us, whether of mind or of body.

If we do this repeatedly, it may be that we shall be released from our affliction altogether. Even today there are miraculous cures, both of physical ailments and of the inner diseases of the heart. In these cases clear and dramatic transformations have taken place, wrought by the Spirit of God. But very often we may be obliged, like St Paul, to continue carrying our burden. If God does not consent to take it away, that can only be because we need it. Through it we are humbled, and forced to rely on God rather than on ourselves. This lesson may take a long time to be driven home; the penny may take a long time to drop. Many falls, failures and humiliations may occur until we learn to 'make our weaknesses our special boast', to turn a negative into a positive, an obstacle into a means of progress. But if we persevere we shall learn ultimately to draw on the strength of God, when, as Meister Eckhart put it, 'What is most earthy in us is what helps us most.'

What has been said so far does not exhaust the mystery of transformation which is at the heart of the vow of *conversatio morum*, but perhaps it opens a door whereby we can enter and begin to explore it for ourselves. Meanwhile we must turn our attention to the third vow, the vow of Obedience.

CHAPTER 4

OBEDIENCE

OBEDIENCE IS NOT a popular word today. It strikes a chill into the heart. It makes us think of harsh, tyrannical authority, of power abused, of servile and grovelling submission by people with no self-respect or sense of their own worth. Yet if instead of saying obedience we say love, what a different reaction! Smiles break out immediately, because we all know that love is what we need, what we are looking for continually.

We do not see love and obedience as being connected to each other. Rather we think of obedience as being the negation of love. We only obey people when we have to, out of fear, out of respect for superior strength; it is not something we want to do, and given the choice we would prefer not to do it. Love, on the other hand, springs from free will and desire. Any element of fear or compulsion would corrode and undermine it. We love freely and willingly, and would not wish to do otherwise.

St Benedict, however, does not see things in this way at all. Obedience in his view is not the negation of love; it is the natural expression of it. Obedience, for him, is love in action. He knows that love is not simply a warm glow in the heart or an emotional dependence on someone or something; the essence of love is giving, and if we are going to give generously in all circumstances, then there are going to be times when that will go against our natural wishes and feelings. We may not feel like giving, but we do it nevertheless. Today is a cold and drizzly morning; I would rather stay in bed than join the brethren at Matins. If I do join them, then that is obedience. I have a free hour before Midday Office; I desperately need this time in order to prepare a talk or to mark some essays. Someone then knocks on my door and asks to discuss some personal problem; if I put my own affairs aside and listen to him, then that is obedience.

The essence of obedience is putting others before myself. This means that we obey everyone, not only those who are placed in authority over us. In this sense it is not a virtue peculiar to monasteries but is an indispensable ingredient in all human relations. A mother obeys her child by getting up in the middle of the night to feed it or to quieten its crying. A father obeys his family by going out to work, often very uncongenial work, in order to provide for them. Obedience to superiors, to people in authority is only an extension of the same principle. Hence St Benedict says that monks should not only obey their abbot, but should also obey each other. It is obedience that binds the monastic community together. It is love in action.

Seen in this way, I do not think that many people will have much difficulty with it. As an expression of love, it cannot be harsh, servile or oppressive. But that is only true when we are talking about obedience to our equals, or to people dependent on us. The situation changes once we are required to obey superiors, people invested with authority over us. It is not so easy to see this kind of obedience as an expression of love. How can it be? If an abbot has power over me, then surely my obedience to him is bound to contain some element of fear and compulsion, which militates against genuine love?

St Benedict, however, denies this absolutely. He says that obedience is not genuine if it springs from fear or compulsion. Not that the element of fear is entirely absent. An abbot should not be the kind of person we feel inclined to take liberties with; it is perfectly appropriate that we approach him with a certain awe, even a certain caution. The relationship between monk and abbot ought not to be sentimentalised. Almost all modern translators of St Benedict's Rule do sentimentalise it, for they represent him as saying, 'an abbot should strive to be loved rather than feared.' That is not actually what St Benedict says. He says: 'an abbot should strive to be loved more than feared.' There is no suggestion here that the abbot should not be feared at all, although that is what we today might prefer to be told. There is some fear in the relationship, but it should not predominate.

Above all, it should not be the motive for our obedience, which has quite a different basis. A monk obeys his abbot, not out of fear or compulsion, but out of love for God. He believes that in obeying his abbot he is obeying God. The Will of God is expressed to him through his abbot. By obeying he is therefore purifying himself and advancing along the road to union with God, which is the goal of monastic life. True obedience has a motivation which is entirely spiritual.

Because it is spiritual it is founded on faith. Indeed, how could it be otherwise? An abbot is an ordinary human being, with his own limitations of character and understanding. At times he is bound to make mistakes. How, then, can we take his orders as coming from God? Only faith can lead us to do so. Therefore St Benedict says that the abbot must be obeyed because he is believed to occupy the place of Christ in the monastery. That word 'believed' is crucial. Yet St Benedict is perfectly realistic about abbots and their human limitations. He knows they can make errors of judgment and order things which are not quite right, at any rate in the short term. But because the abbot occupies the place of Christ in the monastery, then the monk who obeys him is obeying God, and in the long term all will work out for the best. By his obedience the monk will be purified from self-will, and this will bring him closer to union with God. Any disadvantages which may result from an erroneous decision on the abbot's part will eventually be neutralised and compensated for by God's providence. So the monk obeys, and waits in faith and patience for God's Will to work itself out. Motivated as he is by faith and love of God, there is nothing servile or fearful about his obedience.

Neither is there any element of compulsion about it. The monk who obeys his abbot does so because he has freely chosen to do so. No-one is forcing him. Indeed this, for St Benedict, is part of what defines a monk. He describes monks as people who live in communities and want to have an abbot over them. Their obedience is freely chosen, and springs from love for God. Any other motivation vitiates the vow and robs it of all spiritual value.

For us moderns, lacking in faith, all this can sound rather frightening. We have a strong sense today of human dignity, and deep down we cannot see why any human being should be entitled to order anyone else around. We also have a strong sense of human rights. The defence of human rights is even seen by some Christians as being the main rôle of the Church in the modern world. Surely both our rights and our dignity are undermined by obedience as St Benedict conceives it?

THE PATH OF LIFE

Was Nietsche not right, after all, when he despised Christianity for advocating slave virtues?

As for human dignity, this cannot be imperilled if we obey out of love for God. As for human rights, we may well ask whether such a notion is a truly Christian one and does not rather reflect the values of secular humanism which predominate in our time. Certainly the monastic community as St Benedict sees it is not based upon this idea. Monks do not have <u>rights</u>, but they do have <u>duties</u> – to God and to each other. In this way the unity of the community is founded and nourished. A community in which everyone considers themselves to have rights is bound to be aggressive and competitive, as the rights of some conflict with the rights of others. If, however, each monk thinks instead of his duties to other people, then all will serve each other and no-one will need to compete or be aggressive since no-one is neglected. This principle is worked out in quite simple, practical ways, such as the rules governing behaviour at table. The meals are in silence, while a brother reads aloud from some instructive or edifying book. If someone wants something passed to him, then there are certain approved signs he can use to indicate what he wants; but ideally he should not need them since all are expected to be alert to each other's needs and pass things automatically without being asked. If a monk has just had the bread passed to him, for example, then the butter and jam will naturally follow; it should not be necessary for him to make additional signals for them. This is the basic principle which should govern the way the brethren relate to each other: each one thinks, not of his own needs or rights, but of those of others. In this way competitiveness and aggression are replaced by generosity and mutual consideration. Obedience builds up this attitude, and there is nothing about it which is servile or insulting to human dignity, even though it is not based upon the notion of rights.

Yet even after considering all this, we may still feel somewhat uneasy about obedience, particularly obedience to superiors. An abbot who is believed to occupy the place of Christ in the monastery, whose orders are taken as coming from God himself – what an opportunity is here for the shameless and tyrannical abuse of power, for the unbridled manipulation and exploitation of others! How can anyone be an abbot without having his head turned by so much authority, so that he becomes a capricious despot? But in fact the abbot's authority is restrained and conditioned in all sorts of ways. St Benedict makes it clear that the relationship between monk and abbot is not one-sided but mutual. If monks have an obligation to obey their abbot, then their abbot has an equal, no, even greater, obligation to act in the best interests of the monks under his care. Over and over again in the Rule it is emphasised that the abbot is responsible for those he rules, that he is to be held accountable for any harm that comes to them. His duty to them is even greater than their duty to him. This is not mere theory; in practice abbots really do strive to fulfil the exacting obligation laid upon them. If the abbot is harsh and tyrannical to his community, then the brethren will become unhappy and that will make life difficult for the abbot himself. His task is quite demanding enough as it is; he is not going to want to make it worse by stirring up unnecessary ill-feeling. The relationship of obedience between monk and abbot is reciprocal; they serve him, but he also serves them; and indeed his service is the more exacting of the two.

There are many other factors which restrain and condition the abbot's authority; but we need not go into them here. What has been said so far is really by way of introduction. Now we need to do with this vow of obedience what we have tried to do with the other vows: to examine its outward, literal aspect, then pass on to the inward spiritual meaning. Here again we shall find that the outward observance of the vow does not translate readily into conditions outside the monastery, but the inner essence is important and relevant for all, whatever their walk of life. It is central for anyone who wishes to pursue the Christian spiritual path with any degree of seriousness.

The outward fulfilment of the vow means simply that the abbot takes all the important decisions about how his monks shall live, both individually and collectively. It is for him to fix their daily timetable to decide the hours of prayer and work, the area of enclosure, the time and places of silence, and so on. He also appoints the officials of the monastery and allots to each monk his proper work, doing all this directly or through delegates. The monks for their part are to accept all this cheerfully, without murmuring or grumbling. The abbot's decisions will not be taken capriciously or lightly. For his guidance he has the Scriptures, the Rule, the traditions of the Order and of the Congregation, not to mention those of his own community; he will also take advice from his council, and sometimes from the whole community. In his dealings with individual monks, too, there is room for what today is called dialogue. If a monk finds a task laid upon him which for one reason or another he feels he cannot cope with, it is perfectly possible for him to go to his abbot and quietly and humbly point out the difficulties. The abbot may then appoint someone to help him or even take the task away from him altogether. If, however, the abbot insists that he continue with the task, then he must obey, trusting in the grace and providence of God. In all matters of major importance the abbot's decision is final; there can be a good deal of 'dialogue' and 'consultation', and in modern times especially there usually is; but the abbot has the last word and once that is uttered it has to be obeyed.

In a moment we shall have to look at the question of how far, if at all, this kind of obedience can apply to people who are not monks. But that will only become clear once we have grasped something of the inner essence of the vow, and the time has now come for us to attempt this.

Once again we find ourselves faced with the mystery of transformation, the mystery which is at the heart of all the vows. Obedience, however, confronts us with a different aspect of the mystery, approaches it from a different perspective, so we are covering ground which is both familiar and new at the same time. Such are the paradoxes out of which the spiritual life is woven. In a way everything is different from everything else; in another everything is the same. The One buds forth into the Many; yet the Many are also enclosed in the One.

St Paul gives us the clue to the mystery of obedience, when he urges his converts to 'have the mind of Christ.' It is not a small thing he is asking. He is asking them to think, feel and act in the same way that Jesus did during his earthly life. In other words, we are not to think our own thoughts, but God's. On one level we may appear to be living an ordinary human life, but really it is God who is living, thinking, and acting in us and through us. 'I live, but not I, Christ lives in me,' Paul declared, and he also told his converts: 'Your life is hidden with Christ in God.'

None of this can happen so long as we cling to our own autonomy and independence. We may, in our more pious moments, acknowledge that God is all and we are nothing, that none of the things we are or have are really ours, that all is gift or loan, that we are stewards, not possessors, and that we are to be held to account for all we think, say or do. Deep down we do not really believe this. We want to run our own lives, think our own thoughts, make our own decisions, pursue our own aims. This is perfectly natural; but we must recognise at the same time that it is the root of all alienation and all strife. It is what separates us from God and from other people. So long as we persist in pursuing our own ideas and our own desires then we shall find ourselves coming into conflict with the ideas and desires of others, which are different. There is no escape from this treadmill unless we learn to function on a deeper level than that of our conscious self – even of our unconscious self, which also contains quite a lot of divisive and alienating matter. We have to get down to the deepest level of all, to what the mystics have called the apex or ground of the soul, where we are one with God and one with each other.

This cannot be done, of course, without the grace of God, but that is not a problem since grace is always available through the Scriptures, through the sacraments and preaching of the Church, and through the prompting of the Holy Spirit in the depths of the heart. The problem is with our own contribution to the process, because it is a contribution which we are singularly unwilling to make. We cannot start functioning on the deeper level unless we stop functioning on the superficial level. We have to cut off our natural thinking and willing if we are to think God's thoughts and will what he wills. This is the essence of religious obedience: the renunciation of the false and superficial so as to get at the deep and true. Our situation is like that of a plant, which, when it finds the surface soil too arid and hard, is forced to strike its roots further down where moisture and nourishment can be found.

Our natural mind and our natural will have both to be broken, if the light and power of God are to take over. It should be noticed that both intellect and will are involved in this. Usually in traditional spiritual teaching only the will aspect is emphasised; we are told that we must renounce self-will in order to obey the Will of God. That is true; but it is only one side of the picture. We are intellectual as well as volitive creatures; we are made to <u>know</u> as well as love. If the process of spiritual transformation in us is to be fully effective, then we must learn to know supernaturally as well as love supernaturally. I hope I shall be forgiven if I say something more about this supernatural knowing, since it is so important yet so rarely talked about.

God cannot be known by the natural human intellect, which can neither prove that He exists at all nor explain what he is. So-called proofs of God's existence have been circulating for many centuries, but they do not work; they carry no conviction, at any rate in a culture and civilisation like ours which takes scientific knowledge as the paradigm of all human knowing. Deeply rooted in our minds today is the conviction that only science offers <u>real</u> knowledge, objective and true; religion, philosophy and art only offer us subjective imaginings and consoling myths. Science works through observation, measurement, classification, analysis and logical deduction; and all of this is perfectly valid for dealing with physical reality. It is not valid for spiritual reality, which simply cannot be known or explored in this way. There exists a spiritual world; there are entities and forces which are not material, but scientific method cannot approach them. If we wish to know and explore the world of the spirit, we can only do this by exposing ourselves to it, opening ourselves to it, letting it take us over – yes, we may even say letting ourselves be 'possessed' by it. The proper model for the mind which wishes to know God is not the scientist with his microscope, but rather the flower which opens to the light; the mirror which reflects the face looking into it; the lake which is turned into liquid fire by the sun's rays falling upon it.

Every truly religious person is therefore to some extent possessed since it is only by letting ourselves become so that we can know God. Receptivity and docility are the characteristics of the God-filled mind. We need them in order to be aware that God exists at all. We need them even more if we are to penetrate the mystery of what he is, his nature or essence, or his manner of relating to us and the world. We have to negate our normal ways of knowing, based on observation, analysis, logical deduction, and enter a kind of darkness which seems not to be a form of knowing at all, but rather an unknowing – indeed, many mystics have called it that. The paradox here, however, which not all the mystics grasped, is that this apparent unknowing is really a form of knowing – the only way, in fact, God can be known by us in this life.

This receptivity and docility, this readiness to be possessed or taken over, this closing down of the normal process of knowing, is the obedience of the intellect. On embarkation upon religious life, whether in the world or in the monastery, we find ourselves faced with things which seem absurd and irrational. There will be doctrines of the Church which we can make no sense of. As we read the Scriptures, too, we shall come across passages, even whole books, which appear boring or meaningless. If we enter a monastery, we shall find ourselves obliged to follow certain practices which seem silly or pointless. Perhaps some of them are; but we should not jump too hastily to that conclusion. Their meaning may emerge if we persist in them over the years; and the same is true of all those other elements on the spiritual path which the rational mind baulks at. We have to not give in to our initial impulse to reject it all. Pondering upon these Scriptures, upon these doctrines, meditating upon them, letting their meaning sink gradually into our hearts, is the only way to understand them and thus come to know something of God. Hence St Benedict lists among the Tools of Good Works the practice of listening willingly to holy reading. If we murmur under our breath, 'Oh no, not Deuteronomy again', or, 'Oh no, not Pope Pius XII's Address to the Catholic Midwives', we cannot perceive what God is revealing of himself through these things. We have to bend the mind, humble it, deny some of its normal operations, if we are to know God. This is obedience of the intellect. It leads in time to a supernatural, suprarational knowing. Later we may use ordinary rational methods to express what we have understood, to make deductions from it, and to relate it to other forms of knowledge. This is large-ly what theology is about. But the root knowledge of God takes place in the divine darkness, the cloud of unknowing which negates the natural mind.

There is more to be said about supernatural knowing, but for the moment we can leave it, since we are concerned here only with the aspect of obedience. Having glanced at the obedience of the mind, we need to turn our attention to the better known topic of obedience of the will, which is equally important – indeed, some would say more so.

St Benedict declares that no-one in the monastery should follow his own will, and here he is insisting on a radical change in our <u>motivation</u>. We cannot stop willing, we cannot stop wanting or desiring things; on the deepest level of all we have to say that we cannot stop loving, for ultimately what we will is what we love. All of this is a fundamental drive in our nature, an elemental fire; and there can be no question of repressing it or snuffing it out. It does, however, have to be redirected and channelled, so that God, and the welfare of others, is our goal, rather than some form of self-gratification. For this to happen, we are obliged once again to live at a deeper level than we naturally tend to. We are driven by many different desires, some conscious and some unconscious, but these do not emanate from the deepest core of ourselves, and therefore what we really want is often not what we think we want. Many people spend the greater part of their lives discovering this; they pursue desire after desire, finding satisfaction in none of them, and growing increasingly exhausted and disillusioned, because, in fact, none of these things which they have been pursuing is what they really want. The human heart is extremely devious. In any person at any given moment, a number of different levels of motivation may be operating. For example, I might feel an intense desire to found a leper colony in Africa. My conscious motivation for that, what I think I am doing it for, is the love of God and of my neighbour. At a deeper, unconscious level. I may have a quite different motive, which is the desire for self-congratulation and the praise of others. At a deeper level still, the deepest level of all, there may be a genuine desire to serve God and my neighbour. But this last and truest desire is frustrated and blocked by the more superficial ones. I never find out what I really want, because I am always led by what I think I want; the false and superficial desires stifle the deep and true one.

The superficial desires have therefore to be cut away, and this is done by obedience, where we do not follow our natural desires at all but simply do what we are given to do, accepting that it is the Will of God mediated through our religious superior. We do not worry about whether we like our work or not, whether we find it rewarding or not; we simply do it as an act of service; and that cuts right through all the superficial levels of motivation, both conscious and unconscious. We have not chosen this work, and on the natural human level we can find very little satisfaction or fulfilment in it; therefore we are forced to thrust our roots further down and find a supernatural motivation for it.

The purification of motive, so that all we do is grounded on the genuine service of God and of others, is the essence of the obedient will. This is why in a Benedictine novitiate the daily horarium is often rather dull, the work monotonous, humdrum and unrewarding. Unable to find satisfaction in the work itself, the novice is forced to find satisfaction in knowing that what he is doing is the Will of God. This effects a mysterious alchemy, a transformation of the will from the pursuit of self to the love of God. The work which was boring and tedious takes on a new resonance and significance. Deeds which are performed, not out of love for self, but out of love for God, have an infinite depth of meaning and value out of all proportion to the value of the deeds in themselves, which might be quite small. Also, in the long run, deeds of this kind are more effective. If what we do is not our own but the result of God working through us, then ultimately it is bound to work out for the best. This, of course, is not at all the way the world sees actions or evaluates them. Rather the usual view is that what matters is whether the action is good or bad in itself; even more important is that it should be carried out efficiently, showing that the requisite skill or technique has been mastered. Motivation counts for very little, if anything. The Christian perspective is quite different. Certainly the deed must be good in itself; bad actions cannot be spiritualised. But what matters even more is the motivation. If it is God who is acting in us, rather than our own selves, then the long-term outcome can only be good, and even our weaknesses and mistakes can contribute to it.

If the essence of obedience lies in the purification of our thoughts and motives, then it is clearly something which is as available to people outside the monastery as to those who are within it. The mere outward practice of obedience, of course, is familiar to us all, whether we are monks or not. We all have to obey, at one time or another: children obey their parents; employees their employers; and all are bound to obey the government and the law of the land. This in itself is perfectly good, but purely natural obedience. It becomes spiritualised, however, the moment we offer it all to God, as St Paul advises us to do, obeying our rulers, yet not seeing this as the service of men but of God. If we are obliged by our obedience to actions we would rather not do, and certainly would never have chosen, so much the better; there will be less of self in what we do, and more chance for God to work through us provided, of course, we are not doing something which is morally evil in itself.

Strangely, the practice of this kind of obedience leads not to slavery but to freedom. Today we tend to think of freedom exclusively as being free from <u>external</u> compulsions, social or political. But more important is freedom from <u>internal</u> compulsions, springing from our intellectual blindness, moral weakness and psychological hang-ups. Once liberated from those, we are truly free – even though we may be outwardly living under an unjust and repressive political regime. It is not a small matter to penetrate beyond our petty cravings and aversions to find the still centre within ourselves, the calm lake which is stirred only by the Spirit of God and reflects only the Divine Light. Jesus told Nicodemus that those who are reborn in this way are like the wind which blows freely, coming from no-one knows where. They are untrammelled, governed by no compulsions, moved by the Holy Spirit, played upon by the Holy Spirit like a harp.

Here is a great mystery, yet it is open to all of us provided we are ready to let go of our own thoughts and desires so that God alone moves us. This is the essence of spiritual obedience.

CHAPTER 5

SILENCE

I T IS IN MANY WAYS a great privilege to live in the late twentieth century. Science and technology have made rapid and enormous advances, resulting in great control over our environment, and the possibility of spreading that control even to the moon and certain of the planets. Poverty and disease, though not by any means banished, have been much reduced in many parts of the world. There seems to be a growing sense of human solidarity, transcending barriers of race, class, nationality or religion; and if this can be deepened, there is hope that some viable solution may be found for the serious economic, social and political problems which have afflicted us for so long. A young person growing up in today's world is faced with an enormous variety of stimulating and rewarding activities to engage in – activities which are not by any means confined to some privileged élite but are open to almost anyone who shows some aptitude for them.

Our world, then, ought to be a most exciting and even euphoric place to live in. For some, no doubt, it is so; but not for all. In the heart of many people today, even the most affluent and well-connected, there is a deep restlessness and insecurity, a growing disquiet which refuses to go away. It is a kind of hollow space, a void, an emptiness in the inner core of ourselves which both fascinates and frightens. On the whole our reaction to it is one of fear. That is hardly surprising, since it is not easy to live with an aching void. It makes all we do seem hollow and meaningless; it calls into question our very existence and identity. So we try to fill this void, with noise and bustle and frenetic activity, with sex and drugs and distractions of every kind; but in the end none of these things work. The hole in the heart turns out to be like the black hole of the astronomers, capable of swallowing up anything we pour into it, yet still remaining unsatisfied. It seems that if we let it, it will swallow up the whole universe.

Some have spoken about this as though it were a new phenomenon, unparalleled before in world history. But that cannot be right. This emptiness in the heart is intrinsic to the human condition and must surely always have existed, in every age and in every culture. It may be, however, that it is felt more acutely by us than it was by most of our ancestors; and there is a curious irony in this. It is at the precise moment when our achievements in the outer world are so many and so spectacular that the aching emptiness in the heart becomes most intense and most painful. Nothing that we say or do, neither our art nor our science nor our philosophy nor our technology can manage to quieten it.

One of the most powerful ways in which it manifests itself is the fear of silence. Our modern world is noisy, and perhaps to a certain extent it has to be so. Our lives are highly mechanised, and machines make noise. Yet ways could probably be found of silencing them, if there was a generally recognised need to do so. On the whole, however, no such need is recognised. Apart from a few sporadic complaints about 'noise pollution' most people, rather than shunning noise, seem to actively seek it. How many are able to relax and feel at ease in a totally silent room? How many can study, or drive a car, or read a newspaper, without a radio playing in the background? Every day we see people travelling on trains, or walking down the street, with a transistor radio clapped to one ear, or both ears engulfed in earphones.

Silence and solitude are related experiences, and we are afraid of them both. Silence, especially coupled with solitude, forces us to face ourselves and the emptiness in our inner core. Already in the seventeenth century, Pascal was saying that most of the world's ills sprang from the human inability to sit quietly in solitude. The problem, then, was already acute in his day. What would he say about us, and our modern way of life?

In solitary silence our normal avenues of escape are cut off. We cannot affirm ourselves by talking, we cannot forget our inner emptiness by clinging to people, to activities, to stimulating experiences. Detached from these reassuring supports, our inner restlessness and insecurity begin to surface into consciousness. Negative emotions of anger or fear or desire begin to well up inside us; nightmarish fantasies arise and the inner void, the hole in the heart, draws us like a whirlpool, threatening to suck us into its darkness and nothingness. Not for nothing is our modern life so noisy and verbose. Anything rather than face that black hole within, silent, relentless and magnetic.

Such reactions are natural, but they are mistaken and based on illusion. The inner void which we are so frightened of is not, in fact, an enemy but a friend. If, as we said a moment ago, it is capable of swallowing up anything we pour into it, if it is capable of swallowing up the entire universe, then that means that it has infinite capacity. If it has infinite capacity, then only the infinite can fill it. It is nothing less than the hunger for God, which is an intrinsic part of human nature. Far from being our greatest weakness, it is our greatest glory. It points to the truth voiced by St Augustine in his Confessions, when he said that God made us for himself, and nothing less is going to satisfy us.

If this is so, why, then, do we dread this inner hollowness of ours, which is, in fact, our greatest hope since it is simply our capacity for God? Why do we run away from that which is highest in our nature? It is because of the highly paradoxical and ambivalent character of our inner emptiness. We have the potential to be filled with God, yes; but that is because we are nothing in ourselves. We are capable of being raised to the greatest heights; but that is because of our extreme poverty and destitution. We can share in God's life and being only because we have no being of our own, no identity of our own. We cannot savour the fulness of God's being unless we first savour our own nothingness; we cannot feel his voice thrilling through us unless we first become aware of the tomb-like emptiness within ourselves which provides the echo-chamber for the divine Word. It is frightening for us to have to do that, because it means, for a time at least, enduring the silence without the Word, the emptiness without the fulness, the nothingness without the being. It takes faith and courage to wait in patience for God to show himself and raise us up from the mighty waters, as the Psalmist puts it. The Kingdom of Heaven may be ablaze with light, but the entrance is shrouded in deepest shadow.

Therefore we flinch from it and run away, and we run away, too, from the silence and solitude which makes us aware of it. It is sometimes said that most people in the modern world feel no need for God. I would deny this, and say rather, that the need is felt very acutely, but it is not usually recognised for what it is. We see only the bottomless darkness of the black hole, and dare not wait to see the life and being which will fill it. We scream at the prospect of being buried alive, like a character in an Edgar Allan Poe story, not waiting to see the tomb become a womb of rebirth.

I have always been fascinated by the story of the Protestant pastor who had lost his faith, and had a recurrent nightmare which led him to consult the great psychiatrist, Jung. In his dream the pastor found himself on the edge of a lake, which was at first calm and peaceful. After a while, however, a wind sprang up and stirred the surface of the water. At that moment the pastor was seized with panic, sensing that something dark and sinister was stirring in the depths of the lake and threatening to emerge at any moment. The dream then ended and the pastor awoke, naturally not finding it very easy to get to sleep again.

Equally fascinating is Jung's analysis of this dream. Knowing the patient to be learned in Scripture despite having no faith, he sought in the Bible for this symbol of water stirred by the wind, which seemed central to the dream and held the clue to its meaning. Jung lighted on the fifth chapter of St John's Gospel, which tells the story of the pool at Bethsaida which at intervals was stirred by a wind, or 'angel of God', and any sick person plunged into the pool at such moments was instantly cured. One sick man complained to Jesus that he was unable to get into the pool, because every time he tried, someone else got there first. Jesus therefore healed him himself.

From this Gospel story Jung deduced that the symbol of wind blowing on water was a sign of God's presence and activity about to become manifest and perceptible. With reference to the Protestant pastor, this would indicate that the God whom he no longer believed in, who had become a mere word and mental concept, was about to become a living reality. Needless to say, it proved impossible for Jung to lead the pastor to the point of being able to realise this, still less accept it. He could not even accept that the Biblical story had any relevance to his dream at all, and went away unsatisfied. Jung thought that this was because he could not face the prospect of God becoming real and alive, and the radical transformation of life which would inevitably result from this.

In general I do not doubt that Jung was right to turn to the Bible for this symbol of wind on water; neither do I doubt the accuracy of his interpretation, skilled and experienced psychiatrist as he was. Yet when pondering on this case history I have often been surprised that Jung lighted upon the passage from St John in preference to certain others which might have explained the symbol more clearly. Also the symbol, and the dream containing it, seem to me to have further resonances and implications which Jung did not explore. They are relevant to our present theme of silence and the inner void, so I hope I shall be forgiven for pursuing them a little further.

Order presupposes a chaos preceding it and underlying it. This is true both of the universe at large and of ourselves and our own inner minds. The harmony of the whole is based upon a tension of opposites, a delicate equilibrium which is difficult to maintain. At all times there is danger of the balance being upset and of chaos reasserting itself. In the Bible water, and especially the sea, is frequently a symbol of the primordial chaos from which the universe has emerged and to which it continually threatens to revert. The ancient Hebrews feared the sea as the realm of darkness and death, the abode of the sea-serpent, Leviathan, who represents all that is most uncontrolled and destructive, both in the cosmos and in the human mind.

In the opening verse of Genesis we see the Spirit, the breath or wind of God, breathing or blowing upon the waters of chaos prior to the act of creation. It is a sinister picture, threatening and foreboding, and it comes as a relief when in the next verse God says: 'Let there be light!' Order is imposed, but chaos comes first. In all four Gospels we encounter the story of the disciples out in a boat, far from land. A wind arises and the waves grow violent. The disciples are frightened, until Jesus calms the waves with a word of command. Here again, order is reasserted, but only after initial confrontation with the fearsome possibility of reverting to chaos.

It is odd that Jung did not think of these passages, which are better known than the one he quoted. It is also odd that he did not explore the theme of *chaos* which is implicit in all of them. Often in his writings he tells us that water is a symbol of the unconscious mind, and the unconscious mind is full of threats and terrors. The pastor in his dream was naturally afraid of it, accustomed as he was to live in the more reassuring world of rational concepts. So are we, not realising that the breath of God is blowing upon the water, preparing to utter the creative Word which will harmonise it and fill it with light. Like the disciples, we are frightened by the dark, heaving waves, not having the faith or patience to await the word of Jesus which will calm them. We are terrified at the prospect of being sucked into the black hole, not realising that if we hold on in faith we shall explode from it into a new universe.

It is true, as Jung saw, that the wind stirring the water indicates that God's creative and healing power is about to manifest itself. However, the operative word here is 'about'. First comes the confrontation with chaos, and it is that which we flinch from. We have a lot in common with the unbelieving pastor and his nightmare.

Nevertheless we must not imitate him. The dark sinister waters, brooded over by the Spirit, are pregnant with the world to be, which we must await in hope and faith. Herein lies the spiritual value of silence, which has been seen as an essential element in monastic life since the beginning, and even those who are not monks must find some place for it in their lives. Silence takes us into the depths – the depths of our own minds, the depths of the inspired writings, and the depths of God. There is no spiritual progress without that descent into the darkness. Silence is related to listening. We cannot expect to be able to hear the Word of God if we continually drown it with noise, whether that noise be generated by our external surroundings or by our own minds. The value of outward physical silence is as a support for the inward silence of the heart which is much more important but which is also much more difficult to achieve. It is easier to find a quiet place than a quiet heart. A truly holy person is one who is able to remain inwardly quiet even in physical surroundings which are noisy and turbulent.

There are different kinds of silence, however, and it is important to cultivate the right one. There is, for example the silence of the morgue, which speaks of death and has no spiritual value whatever. I experienced that myself on one occasion when I spent a night in a very old house where no one lived except an aged housekeeper. Most of the rooms

THE PATH OF LIFE

were unused, dark behind closed shutters, and had not been lived in for decades. Though the rooms were carefully swept and the furniture assiduously polished, the house was like a mausoleum, lifeless and suffocating. The silence which reigned there was similarly oppressive. It was not the sort of silence which furthered any sense of the presence of God, or in which it was easy to pray. Rather it engendered a sense of claustrophobia and a desperate longing for light and air.

There are other places, too, where silence reigns, but a silence full of tension and repressed anger. That also, is spiritually null and needs to be broken. Silence of that kind will not further us in our quest for God. Very different is the silence of wild, remote places, far from any human habitation. This has a quality all of its own. It is by no means simply the absence of noise. On the contrary, wild places are full of sound: wind stirring the leaves; the cries of birds; waves breaking upon the sand. Yet behind all this there is a background of silence, which the sounds punctuate but do not efface; indeed they seem rather to intensify it. It is a silence which is deep and calm, yet pulsating with energy and life. It makes prayer easy and natural; and that is not surprising, since it is a kind of icon of creation. As sounds emerge from the silence and fall back into it, we can see there an image of the universe spoken forth by God, and then breathed back into him again.

I have never been able to forgive GK Chesterton for a Father Brown story in which a murderer's unbalanced mind is betrayed by his fondness for praying alone on hilltops. Normal people, we are told, feel no urge to do this; they pray only in churches down below, together with other people. Never in my life have I read such fatuous nonsense. Of course we need the communal prayer of the church, just as Jesus participated in the worship of the synagogue and the Temple. He also, however, liked to pray in solitary, remote places – even hilltops! – so we should be able to do the same with a clear conscience. My only objection to hilltops – in Britain, at any rate – is that they tend to be too cold and windy for me to be tempted to linger there long. In warmer conditions, that obstacle vanishes, and what was good enough for Jesus is good enough for me too. The quality of silence in such places is peculiarly favourable to prayer.

So, of course, is the silence of places where prayer is frequent, such as churches, and religious houses. It is remarkable that this special kind of silence still lingers around monastic ruins, although all regular prayer there stopped centuries ago. Still more valuable, then, is the silence of a living religious community, where prayer arises daily and permeates the atmosphere. The quality of silence which is found in a religious house is often a very good indication of the spiritual state of the community which lives there. All depends on how the community in question views silence, how far they appreciate it, and, above all, how far they are prepared to cultivate it; for it does need to be cultivated actively by everyone. It is something which the community labours together to create. That is why it is not the dead, oppressive silence of the morgue, but full of life and energy like the silence of wild nature. A community which really prays and really listens, according to the spirit of St Benedict's Rule, will treasure silence and daily build it up, knowing that it helps us to sense the presence of God and to open up to his light and power. Without it, the spiritual life of a community rapidly becomes shallow and sterile.

Unfortunately, in some monasteries in Britain and Europe, the observation of silence is not as good as it should be. I suspect that is because the communities in question see it only in negative, disciplinary terms; they do not appreciate its positive value. They do not preserve or cultivate it because, deep down, they do not really see the point of it. To do so would require a radical shift of mentality. How are we to define a healthy monastic life? Is it basically a life of talk, or a life of silence? Our modern mentality tends to see life as being fundamentally based upon talk, which in monasteries is punctuated by meaningless and frustrating periods of silence. We ought, however, to see it the other way round. The monk's life is basically a silent life, which at times flowers into speech. Words are therefore used sparingly, and only when really needed: to praise God; to instruct and exhort; to communicate at a level which is deep and nourishing, not trivial or superficial. Real communication happens when words are like the sounds of wild nature, emerging from silence, returning to it, but never obliterating it. They do not negate it but rather articulate and express it. That is what real communication is: it is articulated silence.

Why, then, is it not always properly cultivated in religious communities? In part this is no doubt due to that insecurity and fear of our inner emptiness, which we examined at the beginning of this chapter. Silence is frightening to the insecure, until they learn to relax into it and sense the presence of God at its heart. Also there is a tendency for us to be affected by the modern obsession with the notion of *communication*. We are told that communication is an essential part of what it means to be human, and we are continually being sold new methods and techniques which will allegedly enable us to communicate better. So they may; provided we have something which is worth communicating in the first place. That ceases to be so once techniques of communication are no longer regarded as mere means, but become ends in themselves. Obsession with techniques tends to create this situation, in which everyone is a highly trained communicator, but no actual communication goes on because we have all become so shallow, superficial and inwardly drained that we no longer have anything which is worth telling anyone else about. Our spate of words and highly developed communication techniques are simply a mask for our inner emptiness and poverty. They are like the garments of leaves which Adam and Eve wove to cover their shame.

From all this it should be becoming clear now that silence and speech are related realities. How to establish a proper relation between them is one of the most important arts which we need to learn in order to live well. It is this problem, above all, which St Benedict focusses upon in his Rule when he talks about silence. He has, in fact, very little to say about silence as an isolated topic, apart from laying down the times and places where it is to be observed. That he understood the theology and spirituality of silence is clear from his insistence on monastic life as a perpetual listening to the words of the master, who is ultimately God. This spirituality of silence is developed at great lengths in the writings of the Desert Fathers which St Benedict knew and recommended to his followers. He therefore feels dispensed from saying much about it himself, since he is writing only 'a little rule for beginners' which does not presume to tackle deep spiritual questions but merely legislates on the basic minimum of monastic observance. What he concentrates on, therefore, is not silence as such, but what he calls *taciturnitas*, which means proper restraint in speech. He understands monastic life to be basically silent; he is therefore anxious to ensure that when we do talk we do so in a way which does not squander or dissipate the treasures accumulated in silence. Speech has to be carefully controlled and monitored, so that it does not become mere froth, or even something worse – corrosive gossip and backbiting.

St Benedict is not inventing any of this. He is merely voicing an ancient tradition that came to him from the Desert Fathers, and ultimately from the Scriptures – particularly the Wisdom Literature of the Old Testament, where it is frequently stated that the wise man is known by the fewness of his words. We are confronted here with an important aspect of spiritual life which we have almost entirely lost sight of in our communication-obsessed modern world. The truth is that the human faculty of speech has a highly ambivalent character. On the one hand it is one of our greatest glories, distinguishing us from the animal creation: hence in the Book of Genesis we see Adam naming the animals, thereby asserting his understanding of them and supremacy over them (they cannot name themselves). Properly used, it also becomes a means whereby we can communicate with each other and with God. On the other hand it can be highly destructive. As we have just seen, it can easily degenerate into frivolous chatter, in which people talk simply for the sake of talking, because they are afraid of silence and of the depths into which it plunges us. It can also lead to what St Benedict calls 'murmuring' – petulant complaining about the commands of superiors, which undermines obedience, or about the weather, or the food, or other transient conditions of life which are inevitable and no-one's fault, since no-one has control over them. Malicious comments about absent people are not slow to follow. All of this corrodes the spirit of recollection, of humble listening, of obedience, of communal unity, of docile submission to the will of God.

It seems that speech has an inbuilt tendency to degenerate the moment it becomes at all frequent. That is why St Benedict, guided by ancient tradition, seeks to limit it. Once our talking becomes compulsive, once we get carried away by it, then we become splashy and self-assertive, seeking to manipulate, dominate or even destroy other people, rather than help and support them.

I have often been amused by the reaction of Origen to this dictum that the wise man is known by the fewness of his words. He was obviously rather embarrassed by this, as he recalled the extremely lengthy and voluminous character of his own writings. His rather neat solution (in his commentary on St John's Gospel) was to say that although his writings used very many words, they were all about Christ, who is the supreme Word, the Divine Word – therefore, voluminous though his literary output was, there was really only one Word in it! An ingenious answer but not very convincing. It does not recognise the fact that, however sublime and unified the topic, mere quantity of words is sufficient for the degeneration of language to take effect. I can imagine the devil listening to Origen, and saying with a chuckle:

> 'Let him talk, let him talk. The more words he pours out, the more he will see clarity turn to obscurity, understanding to mystification – and

the very truth he initially perceived will finally become a lie.'

No doubt the holiness of Origen's life and the brilliance of his mind did much to mitigate these evil effects. Nevertheless, the danger inherent in compulsive speech remains and needs to be recognised. That is one reason, among others, why I am trying to keep this present book fairly short. Even so, I am probably saying too much, since I am slipping into irrelevant remarks about one of the major Church Fathers. That is probably a sign that this particular chapter has gone on long enough.

Therefore we may conclude with a few brief comments. Silence is an essential element in spiritual growth, and it needs to be cultivated. We must find times and places for it, not only if we are monks but also if we are lay people. In monasteries it is legislated for, therefore easier to maintain. Out in the world it is obviously going to be more difficult, but surely not impossible. A little thought and persistence should be enough to enable us to find or create the necessary gaps. Few are better than none. Simply to relax quietly, alone in a room, can lead to a sense of the presence of God. The ultimate aim is interior silence, when we find a deep centre within ourselves which is always open to God, untroubled by the frettings of desire or the chatterings of the lower mind. But more of this in the later chapters when we come to discuss prayer.

In speech, too, we can try to avoid being too showy and self-assertive. We can be readier to listen than to speak, more concerned with drawing others out than with expressing ourselves. I once met a lady who was highly skilled at this. People who talked to her found themselves pouring forth brilliant and amusing remarks, highly perceptive comments, which they would not normally consider themselves capable of. In fact they were being drawn out by her, without realising it. She alone was fuelling these brilliant flames.

Out of a silent heart, steeped in God, freed from the clamourings of selfish desire, a true Word can sometimes come forth, comforting the lonely, healing the wounded, enlightening the perplexed. But then it is not we who are speaking, but the supreme Word, spoken out of the depths of the Father, The depths themselves, however, whether in the Father or in ourselves, are perpetually silent. There is no Word without a silence from which it emerges and to which it finally returns.

CHAPTER 6

LECTIO DIVINA

THE LIFE OF a Benedictine monk is founded upon three main elements – prayer, *lectio divina* and work. No-one will be surprised at the importance which St Benedict attributes to the first and last of these. Prayer and work are obviously essential to monastic life, as indeed they are to any form of Christian life whatever.

Lectio divina, however, is more perplexing. What, exactly, is it in the first place? Why is it so important for a monk? Should it have comparable importance for a person who is not a monk? The answers to these questions are not immediately obvious. There has been much confusion about them in the past, and there is still some today, although in monastic circles, at least, the matter is steadily becoming clearer.

As to what *lectio* is: for St Benedict the term means principally the meditative reading of Scripture and the Church Fathers. There can be little doubt that for him it is Scripture which constitutes the primary and most important material for *lectio*. The value of the Fathers lies mainly in the contribution they make to our understanding of the Scriptures and of the mysteries contained in them. Scripture, then, is what we focus upon in *lectio*. Our aim is to get to know Scripture well, to absorb it into ourselves – or rather to let ourselves be absorbed into it.

That St Benedict considers *lectio* to be a highly important exercise is made clear by he amount of time he allots to it in the monastic timetable. He expects every monk to do several hours of it every day, all the year round, though more at some times than at others. He is determined to ensure that it actually gets done, and is not dropped for the sake of some other form of activity (or inactivity!) Seniors are expected to patrol the monastery at intervals, and see to it that no-one is wasting the time set aside for *lectio*. It is not a task which he is prepared to see neglected.

Why is it so important for a monk? This is the deepest question of all. Once we understand the answer, we shall also be able to see the importance which *lectio* has for other Christians who are not monks.

The Bible, and especially the New Testament, is not a book like any other book. It is a place of encounter with Christ, who meets us in it and speaks to us through it. We encounter Christ in other ways, of course, especially in the Eucharist, which we shall look into presently; but our encounter in *lectio* has a strangely immediate, direct and challenging character which makes it unique and irreplaceable. It has even, on occasions, led people to the point of conversion. Metropolitan Anthony Bloom tells the story of how, as a sceptical young man with no definite beliefs, he picked up St Mark's Gospel and started to read through it. As he read on he gradually became aware of a 'presence', mysterious and powerful, confronting and challenging him. From then on he had no doubts about the reality of Christ or the urgency of his call. I have known others with similar experiences, and I can match them with my own. There was one day when I sat down to do *lectio*, feeling restless and disquieted about my general spiritual state, aware of certain things needing badly to be done and others needing equally badly to be left undone. For the first quarter of an hour I read from the Old Testament, from the Book of Daniel. That confirmed very strongly what I already sensed about my current situation, but it did not give me the strength, or even the will, to change anything. I then turned to the Gospel of St Luke, and spent a quarter of an hour on that. The effect was immediate and dramatic. The presence which Metropolitan Anthony spoke of, was there. There was an end to inner turbulence and disquiet. I not only knew what had to be done; I also <u>wanted</u> to do it; and even more importantly, realised that I <u>could</u> do it.

Christ speaks to us through the Scriptures in a way which is transforming and energising, and is thus comparable to the Eucharist, which we shall look at more closely in a moment. It is surely this transforming and energising effect which Jesus was referring to when he told his disciples at the Last Supper, 'You are already clean by the word I have spoken to you.'

This text is important since it suggests that the contact with Christ which we experience in *lectio* is a preparation for the more mystical contact which we have with him in the Eucharist. In *lectio* we encounter Christ real and alive as we ponder upon his death and Resurrection. In the Eucharist we not only encounter him, but are actually united with him; the mystery of his death and Resurrection is no longer something we merely ponder upon but something which we participate in. His sacrifice is our sacrifice, his mystery is our mystery. The Eucharist is thus our highest and deepest form of encounter with Christ; but to understand it and profit from it fully requires a certain preparation, and that preparation is provided by *lectio*. This is an important truth which was well understood by the early Church but is often not understood at all today.

In the early centuries of Christianity there was a discipline practiced which was called the *arcanum*. This meant that not everyone was allowed to participate in the entire Liturgy. Catechumens – those who were under instruction but were not yet baptised – were only permitted to attend the first part, which we now call the Liturgy of the Word. Once that was over they had to leave the church and the doors were closed. The sacramental re-enactment of Christ's death and Resurrection was considered too deep a mystery for anyone who had not first been baptised and confirmed after a long period of preparatory instruction as a catechumen.

The interesting question is this. What did this preparatory instruction consist of? It was mainly the study of Scripture. Catechumens read, studied, and even memorised Biblical texts, with appropriate commentary and explanation by the bishop, or whoever else was instructing them. Once they had encountered Christ in the inspired word, once their minds and hearts were saturated with its images, formulas and concepts, then they were deemed ready to approach the sacramental mysteries of Baptism and Eucharist. First the word, then the sign – that was the formula.

In theory all that has changed. There is no more *arcanum,* and everyone, even a total non-believer, is allowed to witness the whole liturgy. Yet I wonder sometimes if there is not, in practice, an *arcanum* operating without our being aware of it. Many people today complain that the liturgy means nothing to them, that they find it boring, irrelevant, and unrelated to their lives. Might that not be, at least in part, because they have not been prepared for it by encountering Christ in the revealed word? Perhaps we need that prior encounter, today just as much as in the early centuries, if the sacrament is to be truly meaningful for us. Without that key to unlock the mystery the sacramental symbol and ritual remains opaque. The grace and illumination are there, but we are unable to perceive them or draw full profit from them. We simply do not see what is really going on. I am sure that many bored and distracted people at the Eucharist are in this situation. I have met some who have admitted quite openly that they have never seen the Eucharist as being about the death and Resurrection of Christ. And who can blame them? It is not all that obvious – unless we have been initiated into it by encountering Christ in the word. As in former times, people are being denied access to the mystery – this time, not by closed doors, but by their own unpreparedness. They may not be excluded physically from the ceremony, but they are excluded spiritually since they do not understand what is happening or how to relate to it – at any rate, not fully.

In my experience, most practising Catholics have at least a vague idea of what the Eucharist is about. They have received instruction on it from priests, parents and teachers. I suspect, however, that even for them the Eucharist would have much more meaning if their hearts and minds had been previously prepared by that strangely challenging and searching encounter with Christ which comes through the practice of *lectio*. It is a unique, necessary, and irreplaceable experience.

Here some may object: but why should we have to make the effort of sitting down and reading Scripture for ourselves? Are we not exposed sufficiently to it already, simply by going to church? The first part of the Mass after all, consists mainly of Scripture readings, and is therefore very properly called the Liturgy of the Word. If we are monks or other professional religious, we are exposed to still more Scripture through our recitation of the daily Office, the Liturgy of the Hours. Is this not sufficient for that encounter which we have been talking about? Why should we need anything more?

Here I have to disagree. Certainly it is very right and proper that we should hear the Scriptures read during the Eucharist or during the Liturgy of Hours. St Benedict himself commends this practice, including it in his list of Tools for Good Works, where he speaks of 'listening readily to holy reading'. Commendable and necessary though this is, I do not think, however, that it is sufficient on its own. For one thing it is not easy for us moderns to do it properly. We are conditioned by a culture which relies heavily upon the written word and upon visual media, so we are not naturally good listeners. The passivity and docility involved in listening to a text being read quickly tends to indifference and distraction. I do not get the impression that the average church-goer today pays much attention to the Scripture readings which make up the Liturgy of the Word. They go in one ear and out of the other, unless a skillful preacher focusses attention upon them in his homily.

There are rich mines of ore in the Scriptures, but they need to be worked at quite hard; there are buried treasures, but they need to be dug up. None of this happens, as a rule, if we merely listen to Scripture readings in a passive sort of way, even assuming they are read clearly and intelligibly (which is by no means always the case). If we want really to get to grips with the inspired word, to make it our own, to digest it and to be transformed by it, we need to sit down and work at it for ourselves. There is no substitute for this. At first it is quite hard going, but with practice it becomes easier and more natural. As the Scriptures become part of us, as we come to respond to them readily and see their relevance to ourselves, then they also have more meaning for us when they are read out in church. The Liturgy of the Word, instead of being something we doze through, becomes an effective preparation for the sacramental mystery which follows. Word and sign work together and complement each other.

All this is by way of preamble. We now need to look at practical questions of how exactly to set about *lectio,* how to draw maximum profit from it, and how to solve the various problems which it raises.

First there is the question of time. As we have seen, St Benedict expected his monks to spend several hours on *lectio* each day. In our own century that is very difficult even for many monks, and for most lay people probably not possible at all. The Constitutions of the English Benedictine Congregation legislate that a minimum of one half-hour each day should be set aside for *lectio,* though more is encouraged if that proves possible. If lay people find that they, also, can keep to this minimum, so much the better; but it would be unwise to lay down hard and fast rules about this. All depends upon individual persons and circumstances. Much profit can be drawn from reading just a short passage from Scripture, pondering upon it, and letting one's mind return to it at intervals during the day when not occupied with other things. The chosen text thus becomes a sort of companion, who is with us continually, and whose presence we advert to from time to time, drawing strength and illumination from it. Some skilled practitioners of *lectio* carry a pocket New Testament with them wherever they go, so that whenever they have a free moment – on a bus, or on a train, or in a waiting room – they can turn to the inspired word and commune with it. In that way it gradually becomes their life-blood – it becomes part of them, and they become part of it. Its life is their life.

The question of exactly how much time to spend on *lectio* each day is thus not a matter we can make strict or universal rules about; but that our practice should be a daily one is scarcely beyond question. *Lectio* is daily food; we need the nourishment which comes from it. We need also to exercise the particular 'muscles' of the mind which come into operation when we set about it – muscles which in our ordinary everyday affairs do not get any exercise at all, and therefore tend to atrophy. In our machine-dominated, technological culture, it is easy for us to forget that the human mind, like a church organ, has different registers, some of which are habitually neglected because our modern lifestyle sees no use for them. In the long-term, however, they are far from useless. They are essential for spiritual growth, and without them our lives suffer great impoverishment.

More important still is the question of which parts of the Bible we should read. Should we read only the New Testament, ignoring the Old, or merely dipping into it occasionally? It is beyond doubt that for Christians it is the New Testament which is most important, which speaks to us most directly and powerfully. A page from the Gospel of St John, for example, if we really take in what it is saying, will affect us far more deeply than a page of genealogies from the Book of Chronicles, or a page from Leviticus telling us what ritual to follow when making the burnt offering. Yet we cannot afford to ignore the Old Testament altogether. It is true that it reaches its culmination and finds it ultimate meaning only in the New Testament; but it is also true that the full

81

meaning and resonance of the New Testament can only be grasped when we see it in relation to the Old. We need to read them together, and see how they relate to each other.

A modern reader, tackling the Old Testament for the first time, is likely to encounter much which will seem boring, or irrelevant, or even positively repellent. There are long genealogies of royal or priestly families which cannot have much interest for us, quite apart from the fact that they are in any case largely concocted for political reasons and cannot be regarded as historically accurate in all details. There are minute descriptions of the fixtures and fittings in the sanctuary, and detailed instructions on how to make the cereal offering or the peace offering, or the wave offering. Since none of us are ever going to be obliged to perform such rituals, there does not seem much point in our reading about them. Worse still, the morality of the Old Testament is often far from edifying. What are we to make of Jacob, who obtains his father's blessing by means of a cheap trick, or Abraham who saves his own skin by lending his wife to Pharaoh as a concubine, or Jephthah who offers his daughter as a sacrifice? Then there is the wholesale massacre of the Canaanites by the invading Hebrews, and the 'ethnic cleansing' programme carried out upon the sons of Amalek – the 'final solution' to the Amalekite problem. We seem very far here from the spiritual and moral teaching of the Sermon on the Mount. Yet St Benedict insists that the whole Bible is inspired – not just the New Testament – and that all of it is to be used for our nourishment, as he exclaims in the last chapter of his Rule:

> What page, what passage of the inspired books of
> the Old and New Testament is not the truest of
> guides for human life?   *Rule of St Benedict 73:3*

St Benedict is not indulging here in mere rhetoric. It is not his custom to do so. Both for him and for us there must be some way of reading the whole Bible which will enable us to be nourished by it and to encounter God in it.

The Old Testament will begin to unfold its secrets once we see it for what it really is – the history of a process whereby God prepares the human race for Christ. It is a very strange process, slow and gradual, but inexorable and unfailing. On the one hand it works by progressive narrowing, focussing, selecting and rejecting. Out of all the myriad species of living creatures teeming upon the earth, one species – the human – is selected and made capable of relating to God. Out of all the races and nations of the world, one – the Jewish – is selected as that from which the Messiah will be born. Out of all the Jewish girls dreaming of becoming the mother of the Messiah, only one – Mary – actually becomes so. In all this we see a process of selection, of focussing, of concentration. At the same time, it is also a process of purification. The Chosen People are progressively purified – by the ritual and moral Law given through Moses, and also by the sufferings and calamities which afflict them, when they transgress that Law (as they frequently do). This process of purification reaches its culmination in Mary, in whom God finally comes to dwell in a much deeper way than he did in the Ark of the Covenant or in the Temple at Jerusalem. Another way of understanding this process is to see it as a dialogue which unfolds between God and the human race. He speaks, we answer – very inadequately; so He speaks again and again, undeterred by our fumbling replies until he finally speaks the ultimate Word in Jesus the Nazarene, the Word made flesh. This is the Word we are still striving to answer –

not perhaps, very successfully; but that does not matter, for God's designs cannot be thwarted in the end, and he can use our very failures as instruments which will achieve his purpose.

Once we understand this, we need no longer be dismayed by the disedifying behaviour of Abraham or Jacob or Joshua or Jephthah. These are not wholly admirable characters; but they are not presented as being so; even with their weaknesses and somewhat undeveloped moral awareness they are instruments of God's providence and show the human race struggling to comprehend God and to relate to him. Throughout the Old Testament we see God taking hold of us weak human creatures, moulding us and refashioning us in order to receive his impress – a process not totally completed even yet. The process goes on; we are involved in it; and we shall understand it better if we ponder on the earlier phases of it which have now passed but which have left their effect upon us. Perhaps Abraham and Jacob were not entirely admirable, but neither was St Peter, who later became the leader of the Church. The slaughter of Amalekites by the Hebrews is not, in itself, a model to imitate, and the ritual butchery of animal sacrifices is not a practice we should wish to see revived. But in all this we can see emerging those elements of implacable conflict and of sacrifice which are intrinsic to all serious spiritual life and are most dazzlingly manifested in the life, death, and Resurrection of Jesus. These same elements, in some form or another, must also be present on our own spiritual path. Pondering upon the Scriptures helps us realise how to fulfil this. Even in the Old Testament genealogy we can see the working of God's providence, as in all these succeeding generations individuals are born who are needed to play their part in the overall plan. The key to all genealogies, of course, is that from St Matthew which is read at the conclusion of Christmas Matins, which shows us the slow, gradual process whereby the human race is led to the point at which Jesus can be given to us. The Ark of the Covenant, the Temple in Jerusalem, the womb of Mary – these are all stages whereby God comes to dwell in our midst in ways which are progressively more powerful and intimate. That process of indwelling, too, has not ended yet; we are still involved in the struggle to perfect it, to achieve the goal to which God is calling us. As we ponder on the stages of the process which have already been completed, we can, with God's help, come to grasp the mystery of where we ourselves stand in that process – both as individuals, and as members of a community, of a nation, of the Church, or of the whole human race. In the Scriptures is contained the mystery of who, what, and where we are in relation to God.

When trying to understand some truth about the spiritual life, it is often better to meditate upon a symbol than to pursue some rational discourse. If we wish to grasp the relationship of the Old Testament to the New there is a highly potent symbol which we can use – which we have already touched upon in another context. It is that contained in the first chapter of the Book of Genesis:

> The earth was without form and void; and darkness was upon the face of the deep; and the Spirit of God was moving over the face of the waters. And God said: 'Let there be light'; and there was light.

The waters of chaos are dark and sinister, yet they are brooded over by the Spirit of God; they are pregnant with the world which will come to be when God speaks his creative word. The Old Testament is like that, full of hints and possibilities and obscure strivings in the midst of darkness and confusion; yet God's spirit is continually at work in it, leading it to the point when the Light dawns and the Son of God is born into it, giving it shape and meaning, and the era of the New Testament begins. How can we fail to see in this the outline of our own life and destiny? That dark, chaotic world of the Old Testament is very much our own world, vaguely groping and searching in the shadows, yearning for the moment when day will break. Yes, we have the Gospel, and Christ in our midst, through the Church's preaching and sacraments; but that power and glory is working in a way which is still largely hidden and not fully manifested, though the Spirit is slowly leading us to a higher degree of realisation, despite the turbulence and confusion of our modern world. The process of narrowing and concentration, of purification and dialogue, still continues. If we make the Scriptures our own, soak our hearts and minds in them, then we may, under the Spirit's guidance, develop an intuitive sense of our place in God's plan – as individuals, as Church, as members of the human race – and learn how to align ourselves properly with the providential design so as to further it rather than thwart it. Then we shall be able to say truly, with the Psalmist: 'Your words are a lamp for my feet and a light for my steps.'

How, then, shall we set about immersing ourselves in the world of Scripture through the practice of *lectio*? I would suggest that we spend half of the time we have set ourselves in the meditative reading of one of the Gospels, in which

Christ encounters us most directly and powerfully. We may precede this by reading from one of the Old Testament books, which look forward to Christ, or from one of the New Testament epistles, which look back to him. In this way Christ becomes the axis around which everything else revolves, the radiance in whose light everything else becomes visible and comprehensible. As the days roll by, we should eventually come to the end of the books we have chosen and move on to others. It will be a long time before we cover the whole Bible – perhaps we do not need to – but even if we do we can always start again, confident that a further reading will always bring new light and an increase of energy.

I would not recommend the extensive use of academic works by Scripture scholars in order to understand the sacred text. Scholars are often preoccupied with purely academic questions which are not of interest to the ordinary reader, which do not help us to understand what the Scriptural authors are actually saying about our relationship with God and how to deepen it. Some modern translations of the Bible, however, have footnotes which can help us when obscurities in a text are clarified by recent scholarship. Beyond this, the average reader probably does not need to go.

Read slowly and carefully, pausing frequently for thought and prayer. Ask what this text reveals about God, about the world, about yourself. Do not see it merely as a guide to lead you through the perplexities of your present situation. See it mainly as a place of encounter with the living God, where he reveals something of himself and invites your response. Persevering in this practice over the years will gradually reap a harvest of abundant fruit.

CHAPTER 7

PRAYER

THIS BOOK IS essentially about prayer. It could hardly be otherwise, since our topic is the spiritual path of the Benedictine monk, and prayer is right at the centre of that path – it is, indeed, the most important single element in the monk's life. His vocation is primarily to prayer, rather than to any other form of activity, however good. At first sight we may be tempted to think that this is the point at which the monk's path diverges most sharply from that of the ordinary Christian. How many Christians, living outside the monastery, consider prayer to be the most important thing they do? How many see it as being what their lives are really all about? Will they not rather say to themselves, consciously or unconsciously: 'Oh, all that is for monks. I've no time for it; I've too much to do.'

In fact, however, the monk's life is less different from that of the ordinary Christian on this point than is generally supposed. Wherever Christian life is genuine and deep, prayer is at the heart of it. That is as true outside the monastery as it is within it. If we often forget this, that is because we tend to see Christian life as being essentially concerned with 'doing good' or, even worse, with 'not doing any harm.' This is a great mistake. Our life as Christians is not about <u>doing</u> anything, but about <u>being</u> something. Once we understand, and start to become, what we are meant to be, then we have a much better chance of understanding and achieving what we are meant to do. What, then, are we meant to be, and what has that to do with prayer?

The moment I decide to follow Christ, I find myself immediately in what might be described as a 'frontier situation.' In other words, I am henceforth living on a frontier, a border, between two worlds – between the seen and the unseen, between time and eternity, between earth and heaven. I am at a point, where different worlds, different forms of energy, converge and interact. There is tension and turbulence when the different forces meet, so the frontier is also a battle-ground. It is our task to harmonise and reconcile the conflicting elements, to mediate between the two worlds, bringing order out of potential chaos, pulling together what threatens to fall apart. This is what Christ did, and it is also what we are all called to do. Anyone who does this is a priest, mediating between heaven and earth, a *pontifex* or builder of bridges across the gulf separating the worlds. Because it involves enduring tension and conflict it is crucifixion; because it involves overcoming and transcending that tension it is resurrection.

If I am a follower of Christ, I must be what he is: priest, mediator and *pontifex*. I must share in his crucifixion and Resurrection, enduring the tension and harmonising it, so that the centrifugal elements are pulled back to the centre.

I cannot do this unless I am myself grounded on the centre. Where, and what, is the centre? Primarily it is God, from whom all things issue forth and to whom they all ultimately return. Secondarily it is the human heart, the innnermost core of ourselves, where we are most directly and intimately linked to God. At the centre of myself I find the centre of all things. In plumbing the depths of the heart, I also plumb the depths of God.

That is what prayer is: rooting and grounding oneself in the centre; a descent into one's innermost self which is also a descent into the abyss of God. That is why the monks of the Eastern church have spoken so much about 'bringing the mind into the heart.' Once I am firmly fixed upon that axis, I can bring all the different worlds which I experience – both seen and unseen – into harmony and relationship with it. This is the highest activity that human beings are capable of; it is the purpose for which they were created.

Prayer also keeps us open to the different worlds. Openness to the world of the senses is not difficult at all; it happens naturally and there is not much need for us to work at it. On the contrary, we are naturally inclined to become engrossed in it to the exclusion of everything else. It is openness to the spiritual world that we need to work on, because this needs quite a lot of effort, helped by the grace of God, before it starts to become easy and spontaneous. Spiritual realities have this character: that they can only be known and explored by our opening ourselves up to them, by our letting ourselves be taken over by them. Here religion and magic are very similar to each other. The difference between them, however, although slight, is vital.

The religious person seeks communion with the ultimate spiritual reality, which is God. There are other realities, too, which, although they are not God, are not material either, and are extremely powerful. It is to these, rather than to God, that the occultist or magician opens up. The motive, also, is seen to be different when we compare religion with magic. The occultist wants power or control over the unseen forces; the magician's art consists in opening oneself up sufficiently to make contact with the forces while still maintaining some degree of control – a risky business, which can easily go disastrously wrong. The religious person, however, is not seeking power or control; quite the contrary. Who can control God? If I open myself up to God, that is so that I can become his servant, his instrument. I am not seeking to dominate but to serve; not to inflate my individual ego but to transcend it. Prayer is thus very different from the operations of the occultist; both in object and in motive. The outcome or final result is also different in religion from what it is in magic. If I try to control or dominate the hidden powers, I am likely to end up being enslaved by them. If, on the other hand, I submit myself to God and embrace the condition of a servant, I am mysteriously liberated. The cosmic forces, whether material or otherwise – what St Paul calls the 'principalities and powers' – have no more control over me. To seek power leads to enslavement; to renounce it leads to freedom. That is the paradox central to all spiritual life. It is the secret of Christ's death and Resurrection.

Prayer, then, has this aim in view: that it seeks to keep the channels open so that God can still communicate with us. It maintains and deepens our relationship with him. Through prayer, his light and power can flow into me, and out into the external world through the things I say and do. Conversely, it is through prayer also that I can take my experience of the external world back to God, to be healed, transmuted and revitalised. Prayer is the principal means whereby I become what I am meant to be: priest, mediator and *pontifex*, linking God to the world and the world to God.

My own part in it is therefore more passive than active. It is something that happens in me and through me rather than something I do myself. Prayer becomes really deep and authentic when it is something done in me by the Spirit of God, while I, for my part, simply let it happen and gently remove whatever obstacles may be hindering it. To make oneself a mere channel for God's power, an æolian harp to be breathed upon by God's Spirit, requires extreme self-effacement and humility. This is why Meister Eckhart insists that all true prayer must be grounded upon deep humility. If we surrender, and let go of all our external activities, our preoccupations, and even our very selves, then the Spirit takes us over and carries us into the depths of God. The less we try to control or monitor the process, the better it goes. 'We do not know how to pray as we ought,' says St Paul, 'but the Spirit himself intercedes for us with sighs too deep for words.' (*Romans 7:26*)

There are many forms and ways of prayer. This book is not going to attempt to speak of them all, but will simply focus on those forms which are the mainstay of the monk's life: the Eucharist, the Liturgy of the Hours, and private prayer. We shall need to examine each of these in turn, asking practical questions about how both monks and non-monks can practice them and relate to them. We shall need to ask also how these three forms of prayer relate to each other and what is their relative importance. All this will be attempted in subsequent chapters. For the moment, however, there are certain questions we need to consider about prayer in general.

I said a moment ago that our part in prayer is to be passive, to let it happen rather than do it ourselves, and to gently remove whatever obstacles may be hindering it. What are these obstacles, and how should we set about removing them? Whole books have been written about this, but here we shall have to be content with a few basic and practical points.

A very common obstacle for people like ourselves, living in the late twentieth century, is the hunger for results. Influenced as we are by our consumer culture, we tend to see prayer as a product which we have bought, and therefore we expect it to yield quick results. What sort of results? Many of us when we settle down to pray, do so with a number of unconscious or half-conscious expectations. Since I have decided to give up some of my invaluable time to God, I expect him to do something for me in return, preferably rather quickly. A sense of inner peace and tranquillity, for example, would be nice to have; or a glimpse of the unity and harmony underlying all things. An occasional prophetic glimpse into the future would be welcome as well. Or perhaps some strains of celestial music, or flashes of supernatural light? If none of these things happen, we feel cheated and want our money back. We expected perceptible results in a short time, and because these have not been forthcoming we conclude that something has gone wrong, or worse, that prayer is not 'all that it's cracked up to be.'

Certainly some very remarkable things can be experienced by people who pray very deeply and frequently. But it is a huge mistake to expect these things to happen as a matter of course, or to engage in prayer in order to experience them. If we do this, then our motive is wrong, and we have totally misunderstood what prayer is and what it is meant to achieve.

Prayer, when it is genuine, has only one aim: to open ourselves up to God, to contact God, to enter into a relationship with God. It is the contact and the relationship which matters; all else is secondary and peripheral. This means that prayer is essentially a gift which we make of ourselves to God. It is all about giving and surrendering. It is not about feelings.

93

Sometimes we can have a very powerful sense of God's presence, healing and strengthening. But at other times our prayer will feel dry and barren, full of distractions and with nothing much going on in our feelings at all. It is as though no-one were there listening to us. Our words awake no answering echo; it is as though we were talking into an airing cupboard. Yet none of that matters provided we have done our best to surrender ourselves totally to God during the period we have set aside for prayer. We have made a gift, an offering, and we can be sure that God has accepted it. We can also be sure that he will reward us in his own time and in his own way. It is often not until after prayer, rather than during it, that we reap the fruits of what we have done.

People often say: 'I try to pray, but I can't.' My answer is always the same: 'If you're trying to do it, then you are doing it.' What people mean when they say that they can't pray, despite their efforts, is that they don't feel anything while praying, that it seems as though nothing is happening. But that does not mean that the prayer was not real or authentic. It may be that nothing was felt; it may even be that no words came; nevertheless some attempt was made to turn the heart and mind to God, and that is prayer. However barren and futile that prayer may seem at the time, God hears it, and it will not fail to have some effect, especially if persisted in. Prayer becomes easier the more we do of it, and the more we learn to respond to the Spirit of God. What is hard and irksome now may well become light and spontaneous later on when we have become more used to it. But whether it is easy or difficult, pleasant or unpleasant, it is always genuine provided we have done the best we can to give ourselves to God, and we need not fear that we have wasted our time.

From all that has been said, we can see that it is very important when entering into prayer not to have any preconceived ideas about what is going to happen. It is a leap into the unknown; we simply cast ourselves upon God, allowing him to carry us wherever he wants us to go. There may be times when our experience is one of ecstatic flight, or calm restfulness; but there will also be times when it feels very dry and barren. Sometimes it will be easy to pray, and we shall feel ourselves carried by the Spirit; at other times we shall feel abandoned and plagued by innumerable distractions. But we must not care one way or the other. What God decides to send us in the way of experience is his affair, not ours; our part is simply to accept whatever comes. This, too, is quite difficult, since our tendency is to want exciting experiences and to shun the drab and ordinary. But it is not the experience in prayer which matters, but the attitude of mind with which we approach it; and that attitude is, as we have seen, one of surrender, giving, trusting. If that is there, then all is well; if not, then we really are wasting our time.

When faced with dryness in prayer, it may be helpful for us to reflect that it would not be at all good for us if our experience was always ecstatic or blissful. Such experiences, especially when at all intense or frequent, can lead to an inflation of the ego. When touched by these sharp darts of ecstasy, we find ourselves thinking: 'Oh, this is rather good. I must be a mystic. Is this the sort of thing St John of the Cross talked about? Perhaps I should write books about it.' Once we start thinking like this, we have fallen into the most fatuous pride, and the game is up. If, on the other hand, we find our prayer difficult or tedious, then we are forced to do it simply as an offering to God, rather than an ego-trip of our own.

Our motive is purified; we are doing something for God, rather than for ourselves. Periods of barrenness are very necessary to keep us humble and unselfish. Even the greatest saints, therefore, have to endure them sometimes. Yet God also knows when to give us consolation, refreshment, illumination, without which we would grow weary and give up.

I do not think that prayer is normally a wearisome experience for those who engage in it with a humble and unselfish spirit. If it is always dry and difficult, then we should look at our lives carefully to see if there is not an obstacle there, something which is blocking the road and hindering the action of the Spirit. Prayer, after all, is a part of life, and it is bound to be influenced by the way we think and behave when we are not praying. Problems in prayer can quite often be traced to quite simple causes, such as having eaten or drunk too much, or some cruel or heartless way in which we have been treating another person, or some unhealthy attachment which we need to break. If there is some obstacle of that kind we need to act promptly to remove it, and we shall probably find our prayer flowing easily and smoothly again. If, on the other hand, despite our careful self-examination, we can find no such obstacle, then we should patiently accept the dryness of our prayer as the Will of God for us at the moment, and persevere despite it.

We must always allow for the possibility that the blockage is caused by something unconscious, something which we are not aware of, and which is not brought to life by our self-examination. We need to ask God's help to see ourselves as we really are, and to pray with the Psalmist: 'Cleanse me from my secret faults.' Regular use of the Sacrament of Reconciliation will do much to remove this kind of blockage. Prayer can be a most powerful healing agent, but we cannot be healed until we first recognise that we are sick, and then name the precise sickness that we are suffering from. We begin by acknowledging the faults which we are conscious of, and casting them on to God's mercy. We then go on to pray that the faults we are not conscious of may be brought to light, so that we may do the same with them.

It is remarkable how often the practice of deep and sincere prayer tends to unearth hidden things anyway, whether we have asked for this or not. I have known of a number of monks just starting out on religious life who have been quite seriously shocked and upset by this phenomenon. A monk will find himself seized by the Spirit, and carried into the depths of God to a degree which he would not have thought possible before. Skillfully avoiding the trap of complacency and pride – having been warned against it, perhaps, by his novice master – he gives humble thanks to God for the favour which has been shown him. So far, all seems to be well. But then, immediately after prayer or soon afterwards, someone says or does something to annoy him and he flies into a passion of rage. This unsettles him seriously. What does it say about his prayer? Is prayer not meant to have a healing and transforming power? How is it then, that he has emerged from prayer only to find himself even more impatient and bad-tempered than usual? Does that mean that the prayer he has just made was not genuine, and that he has been fooling himself?

By no means. The contrary is the case. Deep and genuine prayer searches the depths of the heart and churns up the unconscious, so that hidden things, often of a rather unsavoury character, float to the surface. A light has shone in a dark room, so that the dust, spiders and cobwebs have become visible. A stone has been turned over in the mind, so that we can see the slugs and worms which were lurking underneath. None of this is particularly pleasant to experience, but it is important to go through it because it is the first stage in the healing process. We ought not to be dismayed, but rather pleased that it has happened, for it shows that the Spirit of God is truly active in us.

What should we do, then, when faced with these unpalatable revelations about ourselves? Simply face them, and call them by their proper name: anger, lust, jealousy or whatever they may be. Then cast them on to God for forgiveness and healing. Take them also to the Sacrament of Reconciliation – as soon as we can if they are especially serious. Then forget them, let them go and turn to God again. We must also, of course, do the best we can to avoid giving in to such evil impulses or expressing them in our outward behaviour. But we should never, never think that our prayer has been invalidated by them. That is the very opposite of the truth.

Quite frequently, however, we find that what floats to the surface of the mind, during or after prayer, is not so much evil or frightening, as trivial and silly. It is rubbish, rather than poison. I have found this to be an especially common occurrence during prayer in the early morning, whether this be the Liturgy of the Hours or private mental prayer. Silly, irrelevant thoughts chatter away inside the brain and create distractions. 'Oh, it's Wednesday again, so we'll get that interminable psalm about the Exodus. How hard this seat is. The church is cold, too. Just think of all those people snug in bed, who don't have to get up for another couple of hours. Still, they'll pay for it' and so on and so on. The mind is capable of churning out reams of such rubbish, rather like a photocopier which we have set to produce a hundred copies instead of the mere ten which we wanted, and we have no option but to watch ruefully while the unwanted material is disgorged by the machine.

This experience, too, is perfectly normal, and we should not let ourselves be distressed by it. Here again, what is happening is that our prayer is allowing the Spirit to search our hearts and show us what we are really like inside; except that this time it is not our evil which is coming to light but simply our triviality and hollowness. In some ways this is harder to take. We would rather be evil than silly. However, we need to remember that facing and acknowledging our silliness is the first step towards becoming wise.

What are we to do with foolish distractions of this sort? An enormous amount of advice on this topic has been given by the great teachers of prayer down the Christian centuries. The anonymous fourteenth century author of *The Cloud of Unknowing,* for example, tells us to 'glance over the shoulder' of the distractions, not letting the mind rest in them but gently detaching from them and turning back to God – brushing them away continually, as though they were irritating flies. That counsel has been echoed by many other spiritual guides, before and since. Certainly I think it is important for us not to let ourselves get angry and exasperated because of distractions in prayer, for that only makes things worse. A gentle, rueful, slightly humorous detachment from this mental rubbish is the best attitude to take. Abbot Chapman advises us to watch the silly chatterings of our minds 'with a kind of amused pity.' That is well said. Forcible repression by a strenuous act of will is not usually the best remedy in such circumstances, but rather a sad, smiling recognition of the situation as it really is, and a renewed surrender to God. Even when assailed by impulses which are actually evil, or temptations which are very violent, it is best not to try to fight them ourselves, but simply relax, go loose, and surrender to God, letting him do the fighting. This was what Moses told the Hebrews to do when they saw themselves pursued by the Egyptian army: 'The Lord will fight for you, and you have only to be still.' (*Exodus 14:14.*)

There are, of course, certain forms of prayer which by their very nature tend to stabilise the mind and reduce distraction. We shall look at these later, in the chapters devoted to them – particularly the chapters concerning the Divine Office and private prayer. But for the moment we should note that it is very important for us to avoid becoming obsessed with 'techniques' and 'methods' – a tendency which is extremely strong in our technological culture. There is no technique which of itself guarantees union with God, any more than there is any sex manual which of itself is capable of producing harmony and compatibility between marriage partners. What we are trying to build in our prayer is a relationship, and that is not a matter of technique but of love, trust, surrender and giving. Otherwise what we are calling prayer is simply a kind of mental therapy, aimed at calming the mind and reducing tension. It is self-centred and not God-centred; which means that it is not really prayer at all.

The spirit of surrender and of self-giving is the essence of prayer. Allied to it and inseparable from it is the realisation that prayer is self-validating and does not need justifying in terms of something outside itself. It is not a means to an end; it is itself its own end. In prayer we are relating to God, and there is nothing greater or more important than that. The moment we say this, we realise that it is true and even rather obvious; yet in practice we can easily forget it. Our tendency is to see prayer as a means to some end, and to justify it in terms of that end. Sometimes we enter into prayer in the hope that it will lead to some sort of blissful or exciting experience, as we saw earlier in this chapter. But another common tendency is for us to see prayer as providing us with fuel for other forms of activity. Many people, consciously or otherwise, think that their work and their other various activities are what matters in their life, and that prayer merely provides the energy needed to pursue these activities. Work is the end, prayer the means. But this is quite wrong. Our prayer is the most important thing we do, and our work, if truly unselfish and spiritual, flows out of it and back into it. We might even say that the value of our work lies in the fact that it tests the quality of our prayer. If we are generous, patient and unselfish in our work, then that shows that our prayer has been deep and genuine. It was in our prayer that we learned the unselfishness which is now flowing out into our work.

We enter into prayer simply for the sake of praying, simply for the relationship with God which it establishes. Experiences of various kinds, whether pleasant or unpleasant, are of no importance. Even the healing and transforming effects of prayer, real and important though they are, should not be the reason why we pray. We pray simply for the sake of praying, not for the sake of any results which may follow from it.

Prayer is a leap into the dark. It is casting oneself into an abyss; it is 'running naked into the sea' as Ruysbroeck puts it. We let ourselves drop into the fast-flowing current of the Holy Spirit, without knowing or caring where it will carry us.

Prayer is the greatest of all adventures; it is a journey or voyage; a quest, fascinating and unpredictable, because it leads us into the supreme mystery which is the mystery of God. In prayer we lose all and find all. It is both the journey, food for the journey, and the journey's end.

All that has been said so far refers to prayer in general, and is therefore valid for all the different forms which prayer can take, such as the Eucharist, The Divine Office, and private, personal prayer. We must now, however, examine each of these forms in turn, in order to see how they relate to each other and how best to practice them. We shall start with the Eucharist, since this is the centre of our life as Christians. Once we have understood this, everything else will naturally fall into place.

CHAPTER 8

THE EUCHARIST

WE COME NOW to the most central and important form of Christian prayer. At this point the path of the monk and the path of the non-monk converge. The Eucharist is central to the life of any Christian, whether in the monastery or outside it. It is potentially the greatest source of spiritual strength which we have available to us, since it is the sacrament of unity, linking us to God and to each other. At the same time it has often been misused and misunderstood, with appalling consequences. Some have valued it so highly that they have been prepared to die for it; yet it has also led to bitter strife and wrangling and religious wars. These last are not likely to be repeated in our own day – although acrimonious disputes about the proper manner of celebrating the Eucharist can still occur in religious communities – but there is, nevertheless, a problem of indifference, a complaint about staleness, monotony, and irrelevance, which is common enough in the modern world. This is an obstacle which we must face and learn to overcome, if this greatest of all sacraments is to have the fully illuminating and energising effect upon our lives that it is capable of.

The purpose of this present chapter, therefore, is entirely practical. Volumes have been written about the theology and spirituality of the Eucharist, and I do not feel qualified or entitled to add anything to them. All I want to do is to try to focus on certain very basic questions about what the Eucharist is, what it is all about, and above all how to get into it and pray it.

In the previous chapter, on prayer in general, certain points were made which are particularly relevant to the Eucharist. For example, there is the statement that prayer becomes most authentic and meaningful when we stop seeing it as something which we do ourselves, and see it rather as something which God does in us and through us. This is especially true of eucharistic prayer. It is primarily the offering made by Christ to the Father, and only secondarily our offering. Jesus crucified and risen, lives on in the heart of the Church, offering himself perpetually to the Father for the healing and sanctification of the world. We are allowed the inestimable privilege of sharing in that offering, of making it our own, of becoming the instruments whereby it can continue to be made in our own days.

Certainly there are moments during the celebration of the Eucharist when it is right and appropriate for us to make our own personal and individual prayers, for people we are concerned about, or for our own private needs. What are called the Intercessory Prayers, or the Prayers of the Faithful, or the Bidding Prayers, offer us some scope for this; and we may also profitably use the Preparation of the Gifts for the same purpose. But it would be a great mistake if we were to see the Eucharist as primarily concerned with this. It is not so much a time for us to express our own thoughts and feelings about God, or even to make known our needs to him; rather it is a time for effacing ourselves and forgetting ourselves in the face of a mystery incomparably greater than any of us individually, or indeed all of us put together. The mystery in question is vast and unfathomable. It is the mystery of the sacrificial death and resurrection of Christ, which is enacted perpetually in eternity, was enacted historically in Palestine two thousand years ago, and is projected now into our own time so that we can be drawn into it, become part of it, and be nourished by it.

At this time, then, more than at any other, we should be letting go of all our normal concerns, our private hopes, fears, and plans for the future, and allowing ourselves to be carried by the Spirit of God into the heart of the mystery. Meister Eckhart said very correctly that when approaching the Eucharist we should think of nothing but God. This in itself will do much to overcome the sense of staleness and monotony, of 'having heard it all before.' The words of the Liturgy, the symbolic actions of the celebrant and his assistants, are only a vehicle, a means, through which this most awesome of mysteries is enacted. It is not necessary at every moment to concentrate on the words which are said, or to ponder deliberately on their meaning, though we can do so, of course, when the Spirit prompts us, as he will for some of the time. Very often, however, as we allow ourselves to be drawn into the Eucharist, we shall find that the words are like the repeated prayers of the Rosary, which merely create a kind of background while the mind and heart penetrate beyond to the mystery which is being represented and enacted.

At this point some may ask: but why do we have to approach God in this way? Is not the whole world his handiwork and his temple? Is he not equally present everywhere? Cannot I contact him and unite with him just as easily on a hilltop, or even in a bus queue? Why do we need a church, and ministers, and this particular ritual act? Why not go to God directly, cutting out all this unnecessary and complicated paraphernalia of ceremony and cult priests?

The truth of the matter is, however, that it is not as easy as it sounds for us to unite with God anywhere and at any time. If people who advocate praying in bus queues and supermarkets are honest with themselves, I think they will have to admit that in fact they do not pray in this way very often, if indeed at all. Why is this? We human beings are, unfortunately, very frail creatures, much prone to weakness and distraction – theologians would say that this is due to the Fall. The number and variety of our daily experiences dissipates the mind, and makes it very hard for us to achieve the singleness and concentration needed in order to train it upon God. We need something to help us focus properly. Special places hallowed by prayer, explicitly religious rites and ceremonies, provide us with this. All religions use these means, and in Christianity we have God's guarantee that he will meet us and unite with us in the sacraments and acts of worship which have been handed down to us by the Church's tradition. The Eucharist is the most important of these. God's presence and 'availability' is guaranteed here to the highest degree, and it provides us with a place of encounter, a centre to focus upon, to pull us together, which is much needed in our distracted and dissipated lives.

We should not let the matter rest there, of course. Having found our focus and centre in the Eucharist, having encountered God there, we can then try to do the same thing when we have left the Church and are caught up in the whirl of activity which is called the world. Ideally there should be no distinction in our lives between the *sacred* and the *profane* at all. Every element in our lives, however humdrum or ordinary, is to be sacralised, made holy and offered to God. As Jesus told the Samaritan woman at the well, it is not enough to fence off certain times and places in our lives, call them holy, and make sure that God stays safely enclosed within them. On the contrary, we want the holy to overflow all boundaries and engulf everything. But being weak as we are, we cannot start doing this straight away. We have to begin by focussing and centring upon God at certain privileged times and in certain privileged places. Then, gently and carefully, we can let the boundaries dissolve, so that we really can find God on hilltops, or even in bus queues and supermarkets.

If we surrender to the Eucharist, to the magnetic presence of God which is at the heart of it and is drawing us continually, we shall soon begin to sense its value and reap its fruits. No longer shall we be oppressed by a sense of staleness or monotony. Meister Eckhart once said very pertinently that all things become young again the nearer they approach to their source. That is precisely what we are doing in the Eucharist. We are returning to the primal origins of our religion – the Last Supper, the Crucifixion and Resurrection of Christ. We are returning to Christ himself, and through him to the Father, the origin and goal of all things. We are centring ourselves upon the supreme Centre, the hub of the cosmic wheel, the axis of the universe. Every Eucharist is thus a new beginning, fresh and young. It is, of course, preceded by a kind of death, as we let go for a while of our normal activities and preoccupations and allow ourselves to be caught up in the action of God, swallowed up in the fast-flowing torrent of the Spirit. But out of that death comes new life, as we gain energy and light from union with God, and can return to our normal occupations renewed and refreshed.

This renewal and refreshment is very real, and it is no accident that the basic symbols of the Eucharist are bread and

wine – the ingredients of a festive meal. Our weakness, lassi-
tude and chronic distraction would make it impossible to
become conscious of God or to unite with him unless we
were given help by God himself. It is through the Eucharist
that this help is given. We must try to grasp something of the
mystery of how this happens, though we can only scratch the
surface of it in this present life. When Christ died and rose
again, an immense flood of spiritual light and power was
released into the world. It is through the Eucharist that we are
enabled to tap into that light and power, to draw upon it and
be strengthened by it. Our habitual weakness and blindness
are thus no longer an insuperable obstacle preventing us from
uniting with God. Our weakness is united with that of Christ
and nailed with him to the cross, sharing in his death. Then
the power and light of the Resurrection flows into us
and carries us far beyond what our natural power would be
capable of. It carries us into the abyss of God, the everlasting
silence and mystery at the heart of all things.

The Eucharist is thus above all else the mystical sacrament. We
must consider for a moment what this means. Words like
'mysticism' and 'mystical' are often used very loosely today,
and carry connotations which we do not want here. We are
not concerned with telepathy, clairvoyance, prophetic
glimpses into the future, Tarot cards or astrology. The Church
has traditionally used the word mysticism in a different and
deeper sense. Mysticism is about uniting with God. A mystic
is one who has a strong sense of the reality of God, and whose
mind and will have been swallowed up into God. Mystical
theology is that branch of theology which treats of union
with God, what this means, how and why it is possible, and
also, very importantly, what conditions need to be fulfilled in

order to bring it about. Even so, many people reading this statement will be left feeling that mysticism is not for them. It is for advanced souls, for professional religious. But if we reflect for a moment we shall see immediately that this cannot possibly be so. Union with God is not a secondary element in our religion, nor some kind of 'optional extra.' It is what our religion is all about. Every Christian who prays frequently and sincerely, and who strives to live a generous and unselfish life, is to some degree a mystic. Not all will be granted the ecstatic experiences of St Teresa of Avila or St John of the Cross. But some awareness of the reality of God, and some sense of God's closeness to us, is possible for quite ordinary people, and is far commoner than is generally realised. How deep it is and how far it goes depends upon God's grace and upon the extent to which we are able to surrender to the action of God within us, putting aside our own feelings, preferences, personal ambitions, and so on. But if we are genuinely religious at all, then we already enjoy a certain degree of union with God, and the way towards deepening and strengthening it is always open. This is truly 'the path of life' of which the Psalmist speaks, and which has provided the title for this book.

The Eucharist is the sacrament of union. It is at once the symbol of that union, and also the primary means by which it is effected. It draws us into union with God and with each other. The Fathers of the early Church used to ponder and reflect upon the symbolism of the Eucharist in a way which we have forgotten today. The innumerable ears of corn growing in a wheat-field have been ground into flour and made into a single loaf. Here we have a clear and telling symbol of the Many reduced to One. Our many warring desires have been harmonised and brought into union with God. Our different lives, personalities and preoccupations have been broken down and melted into a single desire, so in the Eucharist we are united with each other. The union which we have with each other in the Eucharist is a mystical, spiritual union which far transcends our superficial and largely sentimental notion of 'fellowship' or 'togetherness.' We are united to each other in God; our union with each other is grounded upon our union with God.

In all this there is a very real element of sacrifice, but also of nourishment and of ecstasy. The different ears of corn have to be ground down in order to become flour for the eucharistic loaf. So, too, our selfish preoccupations and desires have to be ground down, have to die, so that the mystical union can be brought about. We cannot be mystics drowned in God, nor members of the Christian body, the Christian community, so long as we cling to our own egos, our own personalities, our own desires, or any of the things which separate us from each other and from God. We have to let go of all that, nailing it to the cross together with the crucified Christ whose death we re-enact. But this sacrifice leads to nourishment and strength. The flour, once ground down, becomes bread which is food. United with God and with each other, we can draw strength from that union. From God we draw strength which is everlasting and unfailing. A genuinely united community also, is a continual source of strength for its various members, who support and help each other, so that no-one is forced to 'go it alone' in a self-enclosed, atomistic, excessively individualised way of living.

To let go of selfish and individualistic living is also liberating and joyful. Hence the symbolism of wine which is so important in the Eucharist. Like the symbol of bread, the symbol of wine carries the idea of the Many brought back to the One, as we think of the many grapes crushed in order to make the one drink. Wine, however, does not, like bread, suggest nourishment but rather intoxication and ecstasy, and has therefore been used in this sense by many other religions besides Christianity. Such intoxication and ecstasy, moreover, is not by any means just a fanciful notion nor a pleasantly entertaining idea, but a reality which all can experience who are prepared to let go of self. If I surrender my limited ideas and petty self-will and unite instead with the Will of God, if I cast aside my personal prejudices and preferences in order to unite with a community, then I shall soon know the experience of ecstasy. The word ecstasy, means, etymologically, standing outside oneself, rising above oneself. This, when genuinely and sincerely done, brings an inner peace and happiness which cannot be conceived by people who have never tried it.

All this is extremely relevant in a practical, concrete way whenever we settle down to celebrate the Eucharist. Once we bear in mind what we are about, the awesome depth of it all, the immense benefits to be gained from it, and the total surrender of self which is required in order to reap these benefits, then we can easily overcome that initial reaction of boredom and sluggishness and reluctance which so often assails us when we think of going to Church. There is a real challenge to our selfishness here. We may not like the priest; we may not find the sermons very inspiring; we may not feel particularly drawn to the sort of people who frequent the church; we may not care much for the music or the style of celebration. It is true that we often have quite a wide variety of churches to choose from, and some may suit us more than others, but none will suit us entirely, and in whatever church we decide to go to, we shall encounter things which are not quite to our taste. My own sympathies here go out especially to those with highly developed musical sensitivities, which are likely to be greatly offended by what they hear in most Roman Catholic churches almost anywhere in Europe. Music of high quality is often frowned upon in church circles today, on the grounds that it turns the liturgy into a concert; it would seem that only the banal and the mediocre is considered a viable medium for the revelation of God. No matter; there are still low masses which we can attend without being subjected to such distressing experiences. More important still, we need to ask ourselves what we are going to church for. Are we going simply for what we can get out of it, looking for some sort of 'kick' or 'trip' as typical members of the consumer society? Or are we going in the true spirit of prayer striving to make a complete and unreserved offering of ourselves to God? As we saw in the previous chapter, prayer is not a 'trip' but a gift, an act of surrender. That is especially true of the Eucharist, and the more we are able to surrender our personal likes and dislikes, and open ourselves up to the Mystery, the more we shall sense the magnetic presence of God drawing us into itself and making us one.

After all, there is not much point in our symbolically re-enacting the death and Resurrection of Christ, unless that same death and Resurrection is a reality in our own lives. Every Liturgy invites us to make this identification. We sacrifice our own selfish likes and dislikes, and in return we experience communion – union with God and with each other. The more we do this, the more will the strength and illumination and healing power of the Eucharist flow into us. We scarcely realise the treasure hidden in this greatest of sacraments. Once we take it seriously, and surrender to it, we stir a great power from slumber, which can transform our whole lives and personalities.

As in all forms of prayer, in the Eucharist it is the attitude of mind with which we approach it that makes all the difference. All that has been said so far has been an attempt to express what that attitude should be: one of giving and unselfish surrender, the 'sincerity of heart' which the Scriptures so often speak of. But so as not to leave things too vague and general, we ought to look next at the various parts of the eucharistic celebration, so as to see how best to relate to them and pray them.

There is a shape and pattern in the Eucharist which is in itself revealing, and if we ponder on it a little that will help us to enter into it and become caught up in it. As we have seen already, the death and Resurrection of Christ is what it is all about. This mystery, however, is unveiled for us in two ways. At the Last Supper, Jesus took bread and wine, saying, 'This is my body... this is my blood.' There are two elements here: there is the <u>word</u> and there is the <u>sign</u>. The word spoken by Jesus explains the sign and makes it possible for us to understand it; the sign then enacts what has been said, perfecting it by making it actual and concrete. Word and sign thus work together and complement each other.

This twofold pattern is reflected also in the Eucharist as a whole. There are two parts to its structure: the Liturgy of the Word, then the Eucharistic Prayer following it which is completed by the Communion. Both of these parts manifest to us the same mystery, which is that of the death and Resurrection of Christ, but in different ways. The first is through the medium of the Word, and the second through the medium of the Sign. Both word and sign present some problems for us moderns, formed as we are by a culture which is supersaturated with words, and which has forgotten the language of signs. A certain docility and receptivity of the mind is necessary therefore if we are to open ourselves up fully to what is being communicated.

The Penitential Rite which acts as a kind of prelude to the Liturgy of the Word can be used very profitably for this purpose. St Benedict makes humility the foundation and basis of all prayer. We have to approach God with awe and reverence, and also, initially at any rate, not too casually or familiarly. This is something which is not always understood today, when the prevailing tendency is to emphasise God's closeness and intimacy with us; and some clergy therefore pride themselves on 'taking the spookiness out of religion' in order to make it more accessible to ordinary people. The trouble is 'taking the spookiness out' means in practice divesting our worship of all awe and reverence, so that it ceases to be a religious act at all. Of course God is our Father, we are his children, and there is a bond of closeness and intimacy; but that intimacy needs to be founded upon humility and awareness of who and what we are talking to. It is a curious paradox that we can only unite with God in perfect intimacy once we have recognised the gulf that separates us from him. The Penitential Rite is a frank and open acknowledgement of that gulf. We are weak, sinful and fragile; our need for God and dependence upon him is total. Having recognised this and having cast ourselves upon his mercy, we can then open our ears to the Word which he is speaking to us. If the Penitential Rite is then followed by *Glory to God in the highest*, so much the better: our lowliness is contrasted with his glory, and a proper foundation of humility is laid for our listening to the readings.

These, of course, are always Scriptural, and it is obviously right and necessary that they should be so, since in these inspired writings God speaks to us most directly and powerfully. All that was said about them in the earlier chapter on *lectio divina* is relevant here. There is a certain way of encountering God which is unique and irreplaceable and which only Scripture provides. Once again, we have to be docile and receptive, opening the 'ear of the heart' in order truly to listen, in the sense in which the *Prologue* to the Rule of St Benedict uses the term. In these readings God is encountering us and saying something to each of us. If we listen carefully we shall hear something in each reading which is profoundly relevant to the situation we are in at the moment, and which will also, if we take it fully on board, bring us into closer relationship with God. The practice of *lectio* is, of course, an excellent preparation for listening to the liturgical readings, for it makes our relationship with the revealed Word easy and habitual; it softens the ground, so to speak, preparing it to receive the rain from heaven. If we are perplexed about which Scriptural passages to use for our daily *lectio,* why not choose those which we shall also hear in the Liturgy of the day? Liturgy and *lectio* are thus brought into fruitful contact with each other.

The psalm between the readings aims at transposing what we have heard onto the level of prayer. In the readings God speaks to us, whereas in the psalm we respond to him, helped by the fact that the words we use are his own; they are themselves Scripture. The psalms occupy an important place in Christian prayer, and it is no accident that the Divine Office or Liturgy of the Hours is based principally upon them. This is not the time or place to go into this matter in detail; that will be done in the next chapter on the Liturgy of the Hours. For the moment it is sufficient for us to notice that the psalms in the Eucharist are all chosen carefully to relate to the readings; so as to illuminate what they are about and to enable us to respond to them in a spirit of prayer. If it is Christ who is praying for us and in us in the readings, it is also Christ who is praying for us and in us in the psalm; our part is to surrender to that and allow ourselves to be carried. But more of this presently.

The Eucharist has a certain dramatic character as many have recognised in the past: church and theatre have a certain kinship, which is not surprising when we remember that in ancient times all drama was sacred. Like a play, the Eucharist has its climaxes, and the climax of the Liturgy of the Word is the reading of the Gospel. This is accentuated by the Gospel Acclamation which acts as a prelude or overture to it, and also by our standing up while it is read. Here above all we should listen carefully and attentively, for it is at this moment that Christ speaks to us most directly, and we can be sure that each time we hear the Gospel read in the Eucharist there is something of great importance for each of us personally that we need to catch.

What of the homily which often follows? How are we to relate to that? Some, mistakenly, see it as the climax of the whole celebration. Others, equally mistakenly, see it as an unnecessary and unhelpful extra which we could do quite well without. As Fr Ian Petit OSB has said very well in his excellent book on the Eucharist *This is my Body*, the homily is the preacher's opportunity to expound the Scripture for the benefit of the people, breaking open the inspired Word as later the eucharistic bread is broken and shared out. Ideally, then, the homily should be based upon the readings appointed for the day. Unfortunately not all preachers respect this principle, and we may find that instead we are given a cosy little chat, or a series of personal anecdotes, or the potted history of some saint's life. Yet even here we should not shut our eyes in boredom or irritation. The preacher is a sincere Christian, who has been following his spiritual path over a number of years. He is sure to have his own experience, his own store of wisdom to draw upon and we may well find, if we pay attention, that there is something there which is profitable for us to hear. Here, as in all parts of the Eucharist, we should not be too critical but rather open-minded and receptive, ready to receive and accept whatever nourishment may be going, as CS Lewis says somewhere.

If the Creed follows, there is a danger of our reciting it rather mindlessly. It is meant to remind us of what we believe, and to give us the opportunity to reaffirm that belief. That in itself helps the process of binding and unifying which is the whole purpose of the Eucharist. Although at other points in the celebration we may let our minds go beyond what is said, in the Creed we ought to consciously focus on the words and consciously mean what we are saying. If the Creed is sung, this may involve quite a deliberate effort, not to get preoccupied with musical notes but rather to concentrate on the text. We can be more mystical and contemplative later on, but this is the time for a fully focussed awareness.

117

Desert Fathers such as St Antony of Egypt, and certain mystics of the Rhineland school – not to mention our own Julian of Norwich – have said that the highest form of prayer is not petitionary but consists of simple surrender to the Spirit. No doubt this is true; but not always or everywhere. There are times and places when it is perfectly right and appropriate for us to ask God for things, both for ourselves and for others; it has been a constant practice of the Church since the earliest times, and has the authority of both the Old and New Testaments behind it. The petitionary and intercessory prayers which precede the Preparation of the Gifts provide us with scope for this. We should, however, see these intercessions and petitions in the right sort of way. We are not trying to besiege God with requests, not trying to twist his arm or manipulate him, but rather simply to bring our lives, our sufferings, joys, hopes and needs, to him and offer them – that is, hand them over to him, let go of them, cast them onto him, uniting them with the offering of Christ to the Father. In the Preparation of the Gifts we bring these things to the altar, as it were, and leave them there, to be transmuted into light and power as the bread and wine are transmuted into the Body and Blood of Christ. All of that is his work, not ours; and the transmutation of what we have offered will be more perfect and complete the more we really hand it over, let go of it and do not hang on to it. In this as in all areas of spiritual life, what God does in us is far more important than anything which we do ourselves.

The Preface to the Eucharistic Prayer calls upon us to change gear, to move on to a different register of the mind. In the Eucharistic Prayer, the Consecration and the final conclusion of what used to be called the Canon, we are re-enacting

Christ's death and Resurrection, becoming the channels or instruments through which that Mystery can live on in our world. This calls for total self-effacement, and for letting go of all our personal thoughts, feelings and desires. This change of gear, this moving up on to a higher plane, is what we are called to in the words 'Lift up your hearts.' This is the time for thinking of nothing but God, of surrendering to his action. This frame of mind should be maintained as best we can throughout the Eucharistic Prayer and in the Preface which serves as a prelude or overture to it. We should relax and allow ourselves to be swallowed up by the Mystery, engulfed by it, as though we had cast ourselves recklessly and confidently into a swiftly flowing torrent.

If we really have this inward disposition of total surrender and abandonment, it is not necessary that we fix our attention continuously or deliberately upon each word of the Prayer. The words can be like those of the Rosary, which we recite while our mind and heart plunge into the Mystery which they point to, and which far transcends them. We can, as it were, rise above them. At the same time, however, we need to recall that we can only rise above or transcend something which we have already done our best to understand. At the end of his life the great theologian St Thomas Aquinas had a mystical experience which led him to say that all he had written in his theological works was 'straw.' No doubt it was, in comparison with what was finally revealed to him; but that revelation would probably not have come if he had not previously devote the whole of his life to grappling with the Mystery of God with all the powers of his heart and mind. Having become a master of theology, he was enabled by the Spirit to transcend theology. It should be the same for us with the Eucharistic Prayer. We are not entitled to soar beyond the words unless we have first done our best to understand them. Our praying of the Eucharist will become easier and more meaningful if occasionally we sit down with a missal and ponder on the words of the Eucharistic Prayer, meditatively digesting their meaning. Then, during the celebration of the Eucharist, our minds will sometimes rest upon the words and sometimes rise above them, like a bird continually altering the level of its flight.

Even more, perhaps, than the Eucharistic Prayer, the Communion is God's work rather than ours, for it is the moment when he gives himself to us for our illumination and refreshment. Our part is therefore to maintain the maximum inner stillness and passivity, letting him do in us whatever he wishes. Then, with the concluding prayer and dismissal we can return to the everyday world and pursue our normal occupations in the light of what we have been given. This is a most subtle and delicate art, which we shall look at more carefully later on in the chapter *Making Life a Unity*.

The Eucharist is a vast mystery, and even in a large tome it would be impossible to treat of it exhaustively or definitively. This chapter offers no more than a few suggestions and guidelines of a practical kind, to help us celebrate more easily and naturally. For those who wish to pursue the matter further there is an enormous body of literature, both ancient and modern, which they can turn to.

No attempt has been made here, either, to distinguish monastic liturgy from non-monastic. I do not believe that such a distinction exists. Styles of celebration may differ, but that is a purely peripheral matter which does not affect the essence of what we are doing. The Eucharist is neither monastic nor non-monastic but simply Christian, and in it we are all one.

CHAPTER 9

THE LITURGY OF THE HOURS

OW CAN WE TELL if a person entering a monastic
novitiate has a genuine vocation or not? This is a
problem of spiritual discernment, and it requires the
help of the Holy Spirit since human powers on their own are
insufficient to resolve it. Nevertheless, St Benedict in his Rule
alerts the novice-master to certain signs which point to an
authentic vocation. One of these is whether the novice in
question has a zeal for the *opus Dei*, the work of God. A call
to monastic life is above all a call to a certain kind of prayer,
and it is this which St Benedict is referring to when he speaks
of the *opus Dei*. What is this prayer? Why is it so important in
monastic life? Should it have a comparable importance in the
life of people who are not monks? How can we, who live in
a world very different from fourth century Italy, best enter
into this kind of prayer and use it profitably?

What St Benedict calls the *opus Dei* is what we today call the
Divine Office, or the Liturgy of the Hours. The fundamental
idea behind it is that the day should be punctuated by
periods of prayer. We should note that this is communal
prayer, in which all the monks, as far as possible, participate. It
has top priority in the timetable, and St Benedict insists that
no other activity should be preferred to it. Whatever work the
monks may be engaged in, however important or rewarding
it may be, it must be dropped immediately once the signal is
given for one of the monastic Hours. The Divine Office is the
centre of the monk's life. All else flows out from it and leads
back to it.

'Seven times a day have I praised you, sang the Psalmist (*Psalm118:164*) and St Benedict took that quite literally, laying down that the daylight hours be punctuated by seven offices: *Lauds, Prime, Terce, Sext, None, Vespers* and *Compline.* The last of these, *Compline,* was sung in the dark after sundown, but nevertheless was counted as part of the monastic day since only when it was over could the monks go to bed. As for *Matins,* that was a vigil office sung in the middle of the night so it was not counted as one of the seven daylight Hours. For this St Benedict found backing in another Scriptural text: 'Let us arise at night to give him praise' (*Psalm 118:62*).

With some modifications this pattern of daily communal prayer laid down by St Benedict is still followed in monasteries. Communities with a heavy burden of work have found it necessary to simplify it slightly. The office of *Prime* disappeared some time ago and the daylight offices, known as the little hours – *Terce, Sext* and *None* – are now often combined in a single office in the middle of the day. The common pattern today then, is: *Matins, Lauds, Midday Office, Vespers* and *Compline.*

Before we go any further, however, we should note that this Liturgy of the Hours is not an exclusively monastic form of prayer and never has been. It is the prayer of the whole Church and, in one form or another, has been practised by the whole Church from the very beginning of its history. Monks may have cultivated it and developed it in their own special ways but it has never been their private property. During the Middle Ages and the Renaissance it was practised mainly by clerics but even then there were always some devout lay people who had their Book of Hours and prayed from it regularly. In its modern form, called the *Prayer of the Church*, it is coming increasingly into use by all Christians, whether in religious vows or not. Like the Eucharist, therefore, it is one of those spiritual practices which are not specifically monastic but simply Christian. Nevertheless, since monks have cultivated it especially, making it the most important single element in their life after the Eucharist, they have their own perspective upon it, and it might be of interest for us to explore this a little and to see how those who are not monks can tap into it and profit from it.

Perhaps it will be easiest and most fruitful for us to begin by examining some of the secondary and peripheral aspects of the Liturgy of the Hours. Then we can move out into deeper waters and explore the essential nature of this prayer, what it is at its deepest core, so as to then be able to see how best to go about practising it in the various different conditions of modern life.

When we read what St Benedict has to say in his Rule about the Liturgy of the Hours it quickly becomes clear that the element of 'spacing' is very important to him. That is to say, he wants the Hours to be spread out evenly throughout the day so that the day is punctuated by them and thereby given a certain shape and rhythm. The value of this even spacing becomes obvious the moment we reflect on it a little. For example, this regular punctuation of the day by prayer helps us to <u>remember</u> God and his central importance in our lives. A great many, perhaps all, of our spiritual problems are due to our innate tendency to <u>forget</u> God, to simply allow him to be crowded out of our lives by other concerns. We can even define a truly spiritual person as one who remembers, whereas the unspiritual person and the sinner is one who forgets. Yet the tendency to forget is very strong in us. We are all like the soil referred to in Jesus's parable, where the seed was not able to grow because thorns grew up and choked it – the thorns being the cares, preoccupations and pleasures of the world which obsess our minds so that we simply do not advert to the reality of God nor to our relationship with him. This leads to spiritual death, which means that our relationship with God becomes corroded to the extent that it scarcely exists any more. We have become forgotten by him just as he has been forgotten by us. The person who remembers God, however, is also remembered by him; in other words, the relationship still exists, is vital and growing. The even spacing of the Hours throughout the day is therefore important because it prevents our minds from wandering too far away and keeps bringing them back to the centre so that God is never forgotten and neither are we forgotten by him.

The way in which the Hours are distributed throughout the day by St Benedict also has the effect of giving the day a certain shape and rhythm. In other words, what is happening is that by praying at these regular intervals we are changing our concept of time. We are making time holy by consecrating it to God. Our normal, unspiritual experience of time is not holy at all. Especially for us moderns, plunged into a hectic sequence of different and seemingly unrelated activities, time is simply an indeterminate flux, with no shape or direction. It is not going anywhere, it does not lead to anything or mean anything; it simply passes. If we are enjoying ourselves it seems to pass quickly; if we are bored or tired it drags slowly; so we are aware of time having a certain pace and a certain quality. But that pace and quality do not belong to time itself, for time takes its qualities and colouring from the events and experiences which occur in it. When these events and experiences are deeply meaningful or satisfying a very odd phenomenon occurs: time does not simply pass quickly but comes very near to disappearing altogether. Ecstatic and blissful moments seem to give us a taste of eternity in which time has ceased to exist. When our experiences lack the intensity and vivid colouring, then we become very aware of time and it crawls along very slowly. Our experience of time is affected by whether it is winter or summer, early morning or late afternoon.

What we would like, of course, is to live in a time which was always highly coloured, vivid and intense, a perpetual spring, a perpetual youth, a perpetual sunny morning. Now Meister Eckhart once observed that all things become young the nearer they are to their source, which is God. By continually bringing the flow of time back to God through regular periods of prayer we are rejuvenating it, giving it life and colour and meaning by relating it to its origin.

The distribution of the Hours by St Benedict builds on our natural experience of time and hallows it. *Matins* consecrates the hours of the night, of silence and darkness. *Lauds* consecrates the time of sunrise, *Vespers* the time of sunset. (St Benedict insists that *Vespers* must be sung while there is still light enough for a lantern not to be needed.) The high noonday is also consecrated by its own proper office, as is the period after sunset when we prepare to go to bed. In St Benedict's day these hours were timed not by clocks but by the position of the sun in the heavens. Therefore the time when they were celebrated would depend upon the length of the day and the season of the year and the natural rhythms of the human body. Furthermore, the seasons of the year were given new meaning and quality by being linked with the various phases in the life, death and Resurrection of Christ, the coming of the Spirit and the birth of the Church. The darkness of winter was offset by the Christmas feast which occurs close to the winter solstice, when the days gradually begin to lengthen. As winter closed there was Lent, a period of preparation and purification culminating in Easter, the feast of the Resurrection, celebrated when nature also was bursting forth into new life. The summer months were bathed in the light of Pentecost, the feast of the Holy Spirit, the giver of life.

The hours of the day were also hallowed by the Divine Office. *Lauds* was clearly related to the Resurrection, *Vespers* to the Crucifixion, the 'evening sacrifice' which the Psalmist speaks of. *Matins* could be seen as the time of Christ's resting in the tomb and descent into the realms of the dead until the secret workings of the Spirit suddenly burst forth in the Resurrection.

Our natural, unredeemed experience of time can be oppressive and wearisome, an awareness of endless, pointless cycles of birth, decay and death which merely repeat themselves without going anywhere or meaning anything. This is the experience of time voiced with such melancholy fatigue in the Book of Ecclesiastes, the Preacher. But when time is given quality and meaning by being related, through prayer, to the birth, death and Resurrection of Christ it ceases to be burdensome, enslaving and oppressive, and becomes instead a rhythm which liberates. Through the Liturgy of the Hours time is brought back to its source in the eternity of God. The Liturgy of the Hours uses time in order to free us from time.

In order for this rhythm to have its full effect it is, of course, necessary for the Hours to be prayed regularly and as closely as possible to the proper times in the day allotted to them. Cardinal Richelieu, who recited his entire Office in the middle of the night before going to bed so as to have the rest of the time available for affairs of state, thereby lost out entirely on this aspect of the Liturgy of the Hours. In modern monasteries, also, something of it is lost since the times of offices are fixed by the clock rather than by the position of the sun. Nevertheless, they are spaced out fairly evenly throughout the day so that we still we retain something of that primordial rhythm which St Benedict established. We are still encouraged to remember and not to forget; and the flow of time is still channelled in a meaningful way, giving it colour and quality by relating it to God through Christ the Mediator.

But what of those who are not monks, who live busy, stressful lives in the world, with very little time for prayer? How can they hope to enter into this rhythm of the Hours and draw strength from it? Obviously they cannot be expected to pray the entire Office each day. But they might be able to keep faithful to a certain basic minimum of practice. The Constitutions of the English Benedictine Congregation, catering for monks who for various perfectly valid reasons may be engaged in highly active work outside the monastic enclosure, encourage them to remember 'the particular importance of *Lauds* and *Vespers*.' These are the Offices referred to in the *Prayer of the Church* (the Roman Breviary) as *Morning Prayer* and *Evening Prayer*. These, even if not done precisely at sunrise and sunset, will sanctify the main parts of the day. They provide a basic, practical minimum which will ensure that our day is given some spiritual shape and meaning. As for midday and bedtime, even if we cannot manage a complete Office we can perhaps use some simpler and shorter form of prayer, which will lead us to remember God and hallow the passage of time to some degree. Such a hallowing of time is not a trivial ideal but one well worth striving for, one which is a service badly needed by the modern world. As we have desecrated space by covering the earth with profane and ugly buildings so we have desecrated time by filling it with profane and ugly actions. The proper use of time is one of the greatest treasures in the Church's possession, and imparts great strength to all who have recourse to it. Should it ever disappear from the world altogether then the plight of the human race would be grave indeed.

Was this hallowing of time the only thing St Benedict established when, basing his Rule on previous monastic practice, he arranged for the Hours to be distributed throughout the day? Certainly not; for he also has the idea of a certain amount of communal prayer to be got through during the week, a quota, a measure of service or *pensum servitutis* as he calls it in his Rule. The Liturgy of the Hours in its ancient monastic form consisted mainly of the recitation of psalms, as it still does today, and in a moment we shall be looking at the reason for this and how best to pray these psalms. For the moment, however, we should note that St Benedict expects his monks to get through the entire psalter of one hundred and fifty psalms during the course of a week, and considers a community to be very lazy and slack if it fails to do so. There is, therefore, a certain workload to be shifted, an obligation to be fulfilled, and Cardinal Richelieu, when he prayed his entire daily Office in the middle of the night, may have failed to hallow his time but he had, nevertheless, fulfilled his obligation (which was all most people cared about by the seventeenth century, when the hallowing of time had faded from normal consciousness). How seriously can we, today, take this idea of a quota, or fixed measure of service? Is it meaningful or practicable for us in today's world?

Certainly it creates a number of problems, especially for busy and active people who have to fit their Office into a very packed timetable. The sense of being obliged to a certain fixed quota of psalmody can create a preoccupation with getting it done, so that it ceases to be prayer and becomes a mere chore. In other words, instead of praying the psalms we merely get through them, as though we were peeling potatoes or shelling peas. Even in religious communities today it is not by any means the universal practice to recite the entire psalter in the course of a week. Still less can busy people who are not in religious vows be expected to shift this sort of load. Yet St Benedict's idea of a certain basic minimum which we should stick at – is there not a measure of wisdom in this? If we simply leave the question open, saying at the beginning of each day: 'Well, I'll do whatever I can fit in, depending upon circumstance' then the tendency to drift into laziness, or to let prayer be crowded out by other concerns, is likely to prove irresistible. Monks of the English Congregation are told by their Constitutions to see *Lauds* and *Vespers* as being especially important. Their counterparts in the Roman Breviary – *Morning Prayer* and *Evening Prayer* – ought to prove a feasible daily minimum for most people in most walks of life today, and if more can be done, so much the better. Each person needs to be realistic about this and reflect carefully on what really is possible. Having established a feasible minimum it is important to remain faithful to it. This curbs the tendency to laziness and forgetfulness and anchors our daily life firmly on God, in union with Christ and the Church.

Another basic feature of the Liturgy of the Hours is that it is not private, individual prayer but communal prayer, which we make as members of a Christian community as part of the Body of Christ. This, when properly grasped, has far-reaching consequences. On the purely practical level, for example, it means that it is best prayed together with other people rather than privately. Even if circumstances oblige us to do it without the support of having other people physically present and praying it with us, we need always to remember that it is the prayer of the Church, ultimately of Christ himself, and it is in union with him and the Church that we are offering it.

It is in the light of this fact that we should consider the psalms which constitute the basic substance of the Hours. Why should the Divine Office consist mainly of these psalms? How can these ancient Jewish texts, dating from the centuries before Christ, be meaningful for us today? How can we pray them?

At first sight the psalms present certain problems for the modern Christian. Some of them appear simply obscure and incomprehensible – 'The Lord said to my Lord: Sit at my right hand.' Others express violent and malicious sentiments which seem far removed from the teaching of Jesus in the Sermon on the Mount, as when, for example, the Psalmist calls down curses on his enemies. Even the psalms which express universal human sentiments, such as joy and sorrow, can be difficult at times, since they may not correspond to our own feelings at the moment when we are praying, so that there is a problem of identification. I may, for example, be feeling tired and depressed but I am required to sing, 'Ring out your joy to the Lord.' On other occasions, when things are going well for me I am expected to sing, 'Rescue me from sinking in the mud' or 'My one companion is darkness.' How do we resolve these difficulties, so that the psalms can be a true vehicle of prayer?

First we have to remember that what we are doing is not private, individual prayer in which we pour out to God our personal hopes, disappointments and longings. We are participating in the prayer of Christ who everlastingly, through the Church, intercedes with the Father for the salvation of the entire human race. This is a great torrent of prayer which will continue flowing until the end of time; our part is simply to drop into it and let ourselves be carried by it; or, to use another image, we let ourselves become channels for this prayer, allowing the Spirit of Christ to pray in us and through us.

What we are called upon to do is to drop our own personal preoccupations and put on instead what St Paul calls 'the mind of Christ.' It does not matter in a sorrowful psalm if we are not feeling sorrowful ourselves at the moment; there are always human beings throughout the world who are afflicted with sorrow, and it is on behalf of them, and in union with them through Christ, that we are praying. Similarly, when we see things from this universal, Christ-like standpoint there are always grounds for expressing joy and thanksgiving, even though we may not ourselves be feeling particularly cheerful at the moment. It is a much greater thing to put on the mind of Christ, to think his thoughts and identify with his aims, than to remain locked in our own private world of personal ambitions, hopes and fears. We are invited to step out of ourselves and pray, not as private individuals but as members of the whole human race and of the Body of Christ which is the Church.

Why has the Church chosen the psalms as the vehicle for this universal prayer of Christ? Because, although the psalms originated as hymns for the ancient Jewish Temple liturgy, the Church has always seen them as possessing a certain prophetic character, expressing (though sometimes in a veiled symbolism) the Mystery of Christ, who he is, what he has done and what he continues to do. We know that Jesus, during his earthly life, prayed these psalms daily, and it is in him that their full meaning emerges. It is in this sense that we should understand them and pray them. This is easy to do in those psalms which address a royal or messianic person whom we can readily see as the triumphant Christ, risen and ascended. Psalms of sorrow and dereliction, on the other hand, express the mind and heart of the crucified Christ who still suffers and pleads in all those people throughout the world who are crushed by sorrow. Even an obscure psalm like 'The Lord said to my Lord: Sit at my right' becomes meaningful when placed in the mouth of God the Son, begotten before all ages, and now seated at the right hand of the Father.

But what of the cursing psalms, expressing violent and venomous sentiments? One Benedictine novice is alleged to have said that he found no problem with these; he simply applied them to his novice-master. Phrases like: 'Let him consume away like a snail' and 'Let another man take his office' lent themselves readily to this kind of interpretation. The problem with this approach is that it does not harmonise too well with

Jesus's insistence that we should love our enemies. For this reason, perhaps, the Roman Breviary does not include any of these cursing psalms. I am told that they are not used either in the public worship of the Jewish synagogue. They do occur, however, in the prayers said by Jewish people within the bosom of their own families; the cursing passages, however, are in small print and are meant to be said in a low voice (which must make them sound even more venomous). Suppose, then, that we are praying some form of the Liturgy of the Hours in which cursing psalms are included. What are we to make of them? How can we pray them?

Certainly there can be no question of our applying them to any human individual nor to any group of people, whether racial, national, social or political. That would indeed be inconsistent with the Sermon on the Mount. There are, nevertheless, many forces of evil in the world which darken the hearts of men and lead them to do great harm. (Feminists will not, I am sure, mind my using the exclusive term 'men' here since I am attributing evil to it. That is not meant to imply, however, that women are in some way immune to evil.) Christ, we know, hates evil unwaveringly and implacably, and is resolved upon its ultimate overthrow. This is something we can identify with unhesitatingly; it does not matter what we think these evil forces are or how we conceive them. Traditionally they have been seen as conscious, even personal entities, demons or evil spirits, the 'principalities and powers' spoken of by St Paul. Some people today may prefer simply to refer to them in a general sort of way as the 'dark side of reality', the imperfections and negative elements inherent in created nature. However we conceive these evil forces which we perceive in ourselves and in the world around us they are clearly recognisable as enemies, which we strive to overcome by drawing on the power flowing from Christ's death and Resurrection.

The Jewish practice of reciting the cursing passages in a low voice is suggestive. It hints that at the heart of all evil there is a mystery which as yet cannot be fully understood until the end of time, when Christ's work reaches its final consummation. But this is not a matter which we can go into here and now in this present chapter.

The universal and communal character of the Liturgy of the Hours as the prayer of Christ means, as we saw a moment ago, that it is best prayed together with other people rather than on one's own. This has, of course, a binding and unifying effect upon those who pray it in this way. Religious communities would quickly dissolve into factions and rival cliques if they were not held together by the deep spiritual bond created by fidelity to the Hours. Families who pray it together will soon feel its beneficial effects. Care needs to be taken, however, when deciding what form of this liturgy is going to be used. Most monastic house have their own Divine Office adapted to their own needs. The various lay communities which have sprung up in recent years have also developed their own versions. The Roman Breviary is probably a little too lengthy and complicated for most lay people to use daily. There is no obligation on them, however, to pray all the offices within it, nor even to use all the material within any single office. One could, for example, simply decide to say *Morning Prayer* and *Evening Prayer* each day, using only the appointed psalms and one of the additional prayers. This will be enough to ensure that God is remembered, time hallowed, and Christ's prayer perpetuated in the world.

In monastic communities the Divine Office is usually sung, and there is much to be said for this practice even in a non-monastic setting. This is, of course, presuming that it is being done by a community or small group, rather than by an individual. Most families of lay people, for example, would be somewhat disconcerted if they heard the sound of joyous song issuing from the bedroom of their brother or sister, father or mother. In a group situation, however, the singing of the Hours is much to be recommended. It heightens the sense of the sacred and helps us to be more fully involved, more caught up in what we are doing. Even if we do not sing the psalms, it is important to recite them in a measured, rhythmical way. What matters is not so much whether the recitation is fast or slow; the important thing is that it should be rhythmical. In English-speaking countries we are fortunate in that the various versions of the Divine Office normally use the Grail translation of the psalms, where there is a steady pulse, or beat, to the lines, as for example: 'The Lórd is my shépherd There is nóthing I shall wánt.'

If we sense this beat and maintain it, this helps enormously to steady the mind and dispose it to prayer, even if we are not actually singing. The element of rhythm is a further factor in the hallowing of time and the deepening awareness of the eternal. It is a less peripheral element in the Liturgy of the Hours than is generally realised.

The Eucharist and the Liturgy of the Hours are of central importance in Christian life. In their different yet related ways they perpetuate the life of Christ in our world. Also important, however, is our private, individual prayer, which is the theme of our next chapter.

CHAPTER 10

PRIVATE PRAYER

IN THE SECOND CHAPTER of the Acts of the Apostles the Holy Spirit is described as descending under the appearance of fire, individual tongues of flame resting upon each of the apostles. Certain of the Church Fathers – especially in the Eastern Church – have seen here a symbol of our daily relationship with God. On the one hand there is the single Spirit, binding us into one, so that we relate to God communally as members of a single Body. On the other hand the individual tongues of flame show that each of us has a private, personal and secret relationship to God which is unique and unknown to anyone else. It is important for us to realise that both elements, both communal and private, are needed in order to form a complete spiritual life. They should not be regarded as competing with each other, but rather as complementing each other. If we practise them together they will also feed each other. Our practise of communal prayer will give meaning, direction and focus to our private prayer; similarly our private prayer will give depth and intensity to our communal prayer. As time goes on the distinction between them tends to melt away. Even when we pray in solitude we remain aware of our bond with the whole human race. Even when we pray communally, we may experience something like that which befell the Flemish mystic, Jan van Ruysbroeck, who, during the course of the Divine Office, was often caught up in a mystical ecstasy of the sort we normally associate only with solitary prayer.

There can be no doubt that for Christians, and for monks especially, it is communal prayer which has the higher priority. We are saved communally, as members of the Body of Christ. Those acts of worship, then, which we render as members of the Body are the most central and important. The Eucharist, of course, is the most important of all. By re-enacting in it the death and Resurrection of Christ we tap into that infinite flood of spiritual energy which was released into the world by the Easter Mystery. Unless we are carried and nourished by that energy, we cannot expect to get anywhere spiritually; we cannot 'go it alone'; our human resources are hopelessly insufficient. The Liturgy of the Hours enables us to ponder upon and digest the content of the Mystery as we pray the prophetic words of the psalms and meditate upon the Scriptural passages, all of which enable us to sense the innumerable dimensions, facets and resonances of Christ's saving act and continued presence in the world. The Eucharist is, as it were, the sun, or centre; the Liturgy of the Hours a planetary system revolving around it, receiving light from it and reflecting light back to it. Together, these two forms of worship constitute the basic nourishment, the 'daily bread' of the Christian, whereby the light and power of Christ can flow into us and transform us. The life of Christ thus flows through our veins; his life is our life.

The primary importance of this communal worship, together with the emphasis laid upon it by St Benedict in his Rule, has led some to think that it is the only form of prayer which a monk should practise – perhaps even the only form which any Christian should practise. Private prayer thus comes to be seen as something alien to the monastic tradition, dangerous individualism or heterodox mysticism, by-passing the means of grace laid down for us in the Scriptures, the sacraments and the Liturgy of the Hours. Yet if we reflect for a moment we shall see that this cannot possibly be so. Jesus himself encouraged us to practise private prayer when he spoke of 'going into your own room' of 'shutting the door' and 'praying in secret.' Furthermore, his own life exemplified the principle, for the gospels describe him as frequently praying in solitary places. We are called upon to imitate him in other ways, so why not also in this? Also, our very constitution as human beings makes it necessary for us to pray, at times, on our own. We are both individual and social beings, we have a life which is individual and private together with a life which is shared and communal. A spiritual practice which did not include both dimensions of our nature would be imperfect and insufficient. Grace does not destroy nature but perfects and fulfils it.

All of this is clearly recognised by the Constitutions of the English Benedictine Congregation, which declare that our monks are to do a minimum of one half-hour of private prayer each day. (They are encouraged to do more, of course, if they can; and many do.) This private, mental prayer, as it is called, is taken so seriously that nothing else is allowed to replace it. No other form of prayer, not even the Mass or Divine Office, is a substitute for it. Communal and private prayer are both necessary; neither should knock out the other. They interrelate; they feed each other; and, very often, as has been said above, they flow into each other so that the distinction between them tends to fade away. There is only one prayer, one life; Christ is all in all.

Once we have recognised the value of private prayer and resolved to give some time to it each day, a number of questions arise. What form should this prayer take? How are we to set about it?

There are many different forms of private prayer and we shall look at some of them in a moment. But before we do this we need to recall what has already been said in earlier chapters about the right disposition, or frame of mind, with which we approach prayer. In our consumer society, dominated by technology, we are very prone to become obsessed with 'methods' or 'techniques' of prayer, and thus forget entirely what prayer is really all about and what it is meant to achieve. We are aiming to establish a relationship with God, a relationship of steadily growing intimacy; and this is a relationship with God in which the initiative comes more from God than from us. We talk blithely of our 'quest for God' forgetting that this could never have started unless God had first set out on a quest for us; we talk equally blithely of our 'love for God' though we cannot be sure that it really exists, and even if it does, that is because God loved us first (cf *1 John 4:19*). What we are aiming at in private prayer, as in any other form of prayer, is not so much to do something ourselves but rather allow God to do something in us. We are opening ourselves up to his Spirit; we are surrendering ourselves to his action, letting him take us wherever he wants us to go, allowing him to do in us whatever he sees as needing to be done. Without this proper disposition of surrender, our prayer will have very little value, no matter what form it takes; if, on the other hand, the proper disposition is there, then any form of prayer will be valid and effective.

Our prayer must be first and foremost from the heart. The ground from which our prayer emanates is of primary importance. We need to ensure that it is coming from the right place, which is what the Scriptures call the heart. This is not the physical organ which pumps blood around the body, but the innermost core of our personality, where we are most truly ourselves, without pretence or illusion. We have romanticised the idea of the heart, seeing it primarily as the source of sentiment, and that is too superficial. It is a much deeper reality than that. The heart is that in us which sees the truth most clearly and which wants the highest possible good, even when it is not quite sure what the highest good is. Getting into the heart, into the centre of ourselves, is not particularly easy. Neither is it easy, once having got there, to stay there, to 'bring the mind down into the heart and keep it there' as the monks of the eastern monastic tradition encourage us to do. As with all other aspects of prayer we are most likely to succeed in this if we do not try too hard. Too much strenuous effort on our part leads to the affirmation of self and impedes the action of the Holy Spirit. Rather than digging furiously into ourselves in order to find the heart, we should let ourselves sink into it, let ourselves alight naturally and gently upon it, like a swan upon a lake. The heart draws us by its own magnetism once we surrender, once we let go of all that is secondary and superficial in ourselves, once we let ourselves be carried by the Spirit of God.

Intuition, practice and the promptings of the Holy Spirit will lead us to find what kind of prayer best suits us in our present situation. These last four words are worth noting for, as the years pass by and our relationship with God deepens, the form and quality of our prayer will very probably change. We ought not to try to provoke that change by any deliberate or conscious activity of our own, but simply to be open to it and ready to undergo it when we sense that we are called to do so. From what I have seen in the spiritual lives of the people with whom I have come into contact, it seems to me that change in prayer is usually towards increasing depth and simplicity. The simplicity comes from the fact that fewer words are used, and there are fewer images in the mind. The depth comes from a growing intensity in our desire for God. Unlike ordinary human desire, which beyond a certain point leads to satiety and indifference, the desire for God increases the more we feed it. The more we pray, the more we want to pray; yet there is nothing frenetic or neurotic about this wanting. It is calm, and content to be what it is at the present moment. What is happening is that our capacity for God is being continually widened. A kind of empty space is being hollowed out in the innermost core; a space which God can then fill. The more space there is, the more of himself he can pour in. This is the 'enlarging of the heart' which St Benedict speaks of in the *Prologue* to his Rule, and which he sees as the normal outcome of perseverance in the monastic life.

There is not the time nor the space here for us to explore all the various forms which private prayer can take. An entire book would be needed to do justice to this topic. Here we shall confine ourselves to certain forms of prayer which belong especially to the monastic tradition and grow most naturally out of it, though they are not by any means the exclusive property of monks, and people who are not monks may also find much profit in them.

Therefore nothing is going to be said here about that form of prayer which is common to all believers, and which consists of simply talking to God, naturally and spontaneously in our own words, as to a friend or close relative. There are many occasions, both in monastic life and outside it, when this is the easiest and most appropriate way of praying. The more formalised traditional prayers of the Church recited from a book or by heart, such as the *Our Father*, the *Hail Mary*, the *Memorare* and so on, also lie outside our present scope. Devotion to our Lady is certainly a large part of monastic prayer but it is not by any means peculiar to monks, and is too large a topic to be included here. As for the Rosary – one of the greatest treasures in the Church's possession – a whole book would be needed to treat of it adequately.

There are certain forms of private prayer, however, which seem to have been present in the monastic tradition from the earliest times and are still much practised today. They are not widely known outside monastic circles, yet could surely be used very profitably by people who are not monks, especially if their spiritual life, like that of monks, is firmly rooted in the Eucharist and the Liturgy of the Hours.

Very often, when doing *lectio* or reciting the Divine Office, a single word or phrase may suddenly 'light up' and carry a resonance of meaning which seems especially important. It might be a phrase such as, 'The Lord is my light and my help' or 'I am the Way, the Truth, and the Life' or some other phrase far less well known which nevertheless seems at the moment to be invested with a special meaning. One can, then, when the Office or *lectio* is over, take that phrase away and ponder on it meditatively. This pondering does not by any means consist exclusively of intellectual analysis whereby we try to express clearly, in different words, exactly what this phrase means, in order to draw practical conclusions from it on how to run our lives from now on. It is perfectly normal and in order, of course, for us to analyse it in this way, and we may find that, in fact, we usually do; but we do not stop at that. Rather, the phrase is allowed to hang in the mind, to ring or resonate in the depths of the heart at a level much deeper

THE PATH OF LIFE

than that of the merely rational and analytical. We repeat it, aloud or silently, with intervals of silence in which we let it sink into the heart and communicate to us something of that mystery of God which is beyond the power of words or concepts to express. It becomes for us, therefore, something resembling what the great religions of Asia call a *mantra* – a sacred word or phrase repeated over and over again to settle the mind, to deepen concentration, and to tune us into the divine. We can carry this word or phrase about with us throughout the day, allowing the mind to settle gently back into it the moment there is a pause, however brief, in the fast-flowing current of our daily activities. It becomes an axis, a spiritual centre of calm rootedness around which everything else in our daily life revolves. It takes us to the threshold of what is often called contemplative prayer, about which more will be said in a moment, and which is a far less exclusively monastic prerogative than is generally realised.

We should note that this form of prayer has flowered out of our *lectio* or Divine Office; it could equally well flower out of some text from the Mass. It is therefore firmly grounded in the Mystery of Christ which comes to us through the Scriptures and the sacraments of the Church. This distinguishes it from the *mantras* used in the eastern religions which, though perhaps apparently meaningless, are often the disguised names of Hindu deities or particular manifestations of the Buddha. (This is especially true of what is called transcendental meditation.) It also distinguishes it from the meditation practices of the New Age, or of certain occult groups, where the *mantra* puts us into contact with some 'cosmic force' or 'spirit guide' or 'master' who is certainly not Christ and whose real nature we may not know much about.

144

There are many immaterial forces or powers at work in the universe which transcend the rational and conceptual order, and it should not be a matter of indifference to us which of these we chose to open up to. As Christians we believe that the way of salvation, the path to God, is opened up for us by Christ, and we are in true spiritual security only when we pray in and through him. To try any other way is extremely risky, and for the Christian, an act of infidelity, a kind of spiritual adultery such as the Old Testament prophets often reproached the people of Israel for practising.

Our meditative pondering, then, upon some word or phrase from Scripture or from the Eucharist, is grounded upon the Mystery of Christ revealed through the sacred text. This text conveys a meaning which we can already grasp to a certain extent with our rational intelligence. By the ordinary means of thought and reflection we can form some notion of what is being said about God, ourselves, and our relationship to God through Christ. We know, therefore, that we are within the domain of truth and security. That does not mean, however, that we are obliged to remain on the level of what we can grasp with our rational minds. God is a reality too vast and transcendent to be contained entirely within any set of words or images, even within sacred words and images, hallowed by tradition and the authority of revelation. Once our reflection upon the text has pointed us in the right direction we need not be afraid to go beyond the words and concepts to leap into the divine darkness which transcends all human thought and language – if the Holy Spirit moves us to do so. Neither, of course, are we obliged to attempt such mystical flights if we feel no need for them, and if we are not so prompted by the Holy Spirit. Each time we settle down to pray we should be relaxed, open, and receptive, ready to accept whatever comes, and find by inspiration and intuition what is our proper level at the moment.

The Eucharist, the Liturgy of the Hours, and the practice of *lectio* thus provide us with a firm basis for a mysticism which is securely rooted in Christ and free from danger or illusion. Such venturings onto the threshold of contemplative prayer will also have a vivifying and deepening effect on the way we pray the Eucharist and the Hours. Having listened in silence to what cannot be said, we can gain a more profound understanding of what is said. Then, having pondered anew upon the words of revelation, we can allow ourselves to be caught up once more into the divine darkness. Thus our communal prayer as members of the Body of Christ, and the private prayer flowing from our secret and unique relationship with him, will fuel and nourish each other.

I do not think that for most people it is possible to pray for very long without using any words or images at all. If we attempt it we are likely to fall into distractions or dozing or a sort of mental activity which is not prayer. There is a sort of 'meditation' which aims simply at detaching from the contents of the mind, until our normal turmoil of thought and feelings is stilled, and a certain calm ensues. This can have some therapeutic value, relaxing the mind and nerves; but it is not prayer because it is not God-centred; it is not cultivating or deepening our relationship with him. If we stop trying to pray in a genuine sense and prefer instead to sink into this kind of mental vacuity I think we shall also notice, as time goes on, that it does not change or transform us. It is purely and simply a rest, which allows our life to continue afterwards with some renewed vigour but without any actual change in quality or direction. We shall not become more generous, more patient, or more unselfish; we shall not, in fact, become more holy. Holiness comes from relating, from giving, and such relating and giving is the essence of true prayer.

Another sign which shows that our prayer is genuine is when we perceive that there is a certain yearning or longing at the heart of it. Early spiritual writers have spoken of 'motions of the will', 'acts' or 'beating upon the cloud.' In the Eastern Orthodox writers who treat of the *Jesus Prayer*, the *Prayer of the Heart*, there is talk of a 'soreness of heart,' a kind of burning sensation in the core of ourselves. This yearning is present in all true prayer, including that which uses words, images, and concepts; but there are times when these acts, or motions, or beatings do not seem to need words, and are, in fact, much better off without them. Here we enter the domain of what is often called contemplative prayer – a form of prayer which seems to have been present in the monastic tradition from the earliest times, and finds, perhaps, its fullest and most detailed exposition in the writings of Evagrius of Pontus, who calls it 'pure prayer.' It has often been thought by some – for example, the author of the fourteenth century *Cloud of Unknowing* – to be only really practisable by monks, so that those who are not monks may as well forget about it. Others – notably Meister Eckhart – have taken the view that it is not the exclusive prerogative of any particular profession or way of life, and that anyone can practise it if the Spirit moves them to do so and if they are prepared to surrender and detach themselves sufficiently from their normal selfish thoughts and preoccupations. I personally incline to the latter view. The two 'if's are clearly of primary importance and will automatically exclude a number of people; nevertheless I do not see why prayer of this kind should not be possible for non-monks and I suspect, furthermore, that it is more common than is generally realised. People sometimes drift into it without realising what it is or ever daring to call it contemplative or mystical. It will perhaps be fruitful, then, at this point, to try to describe more exactly what this contemplative or mystical prayer is, and how best to practise it without falling into one of its various counterfeits or substitutes.

It is said of the Curé d'Ars that he noticed an old man who, when Mass was over, would remain for a long time afterwards in the church, seemingly lost in prayer. When the Curé asked him what he was saying to God at such times he answered that he was not saying anything in particular. 'I look at him,' he said, 'and he looks at me, and we are happy together.' This is a simple, clear definition of contemplative prayer; and we may note that it is given by a perfectly ordinary lay man, not a professional religious of any kind, which supports the view that this kind of prayer is not by any means restricted to monks. What are we doing, then, when we engage in this kind of contemplation? We are not asking for anything, we are not thanking God for anything, we are not praying for ourselves or for anyone else; we are not even praising or glorifying God. We are simply resting in his presence, bathing in his light, letting him take us over and carry us wherever he wills. If we use any words they will be very few, and we may reach the point when we sense that we do not need any at all. We simply surrender, hand ourselves over to the God whom we cannot conceive, or understand, or imagine; we drop into the abyss, or 'run naked into the sea' as Ruysbroeck puts it. It is more a passive than an active exercise. The Holy Spirit is the prime mover. Certainly there are motions of will, acts, beatings upon the Cloud which come from us; but these are very gentle, tranquil, unhurried and in no way forced or strained.

We may find, of course, that we cannot remain on this level for long. Distractions intervene, or drowsiness; or we may find ourselves slipping into the kind of mental vacuity which we looked at earlier, and which is not prayer at all because there is no longing for God in it. No matter; if we find ourselves drifting, then we pull minds gently back to God by using some words - either our own, or from a sacred text. There is no obligation whatever for us to remain in the wordless state once we have got there. We can vary, change our mode of prayer continually, doing whatever is easiest in order to keep our minds and hearts centred upon God. We pray with words, or without words, depending on how the Spirit moves us; our part is simply to be docile and responsive.

It is important, too, for us not to become, as it were, spiritual snobs, deciding that prayer in words is only for beginners, whereas wordless prayer is for the advanced. It is a mistake for us to strive after wordless prayer because we have got the idea that it is the highest or best. It is only highest and best if it is what God is prompting us to do. We should do what is easiest or most natural at the moment. Ultimately, it matters not a whit what sort of prayer we engage in provided that in it we hand ourselves over to God with total trust and generosity. If we do that, then our relationship with God will grow, and we shall be progressively transformed by it. All this can happen, and frequently does, to people who have prayed in words all their lives and never thought of doing anything else. A Rosary or Litany prayed in the Spirit will take us

149

further than wordless prayer which is forced and artificial, springing only from our own will.

Nevertheless, there are many people, both inside and outside monasteries, who are called to pray in this wordless way, who need to recognise this calling and respond to it. How can we know that we are being called? The simplest and most obvious sign is, of course, the simple <u>desire</u> to pray without words. This desire is not wilful or forced. We do not decide to dispense with words and then grimly set about driving them away. Rather, the desire for God simply reaches the point, quite easily and naturally, when we shed the words in a relaxed and spontaneous way, as we shed our clothes before stepping into the bath. Another sign that we are called to contemplative prayer is that we find ourselves simply unable to pray in any other way. The moment we start to use words we fall into distractions or a kind of lethargic heaviness in which we sense that we have driven God away. The moment words are dropped, however, we become aware that we are truly praying again, that God has taken us over and that we are responding.

This simple inability to pray in anything other than a contemplative way is described very accurately in the *Spiritual Letters* of Abbot Chapman, who also devised a kind of 'test' whereby he thought he could tell whether a person was called to contemplative prayer or not. This test was based on his own experience, together with the writings of a nineteenth century French Jesuit called Père Poulain. This is how the test works.

See if you can recite an ordinary vocal prayer, such as the *Our Father*, truly striving and longing for God while simultaneously remaining aware of the meaning of the words you are uttering. If you can do this, then prayer in words is right for you and you should not attempt anything else. There are people, however, who cannot do this. The moment they advert to the meaning of the words, they lose all awareness of God, they feel that they are no longer praying. If on the other hand, they stop thinking of the meaning of the words, they are overwhelmed by an awareness of God which blots out the sense of the words, which are recited, as it were, mindlessly, while the mind and heart are elsewhere, drowned in the contemplation of God. This strange phenomenon, whereby the longing for God, or the awareness of his presence, blots out all awareness of words and their meaning, was described by Père Poulain as the *ligature*. It can occur at any time, even during communal and vocal prayer such as the Eucharist or the Liturgy of the Hours. The words of the prayer become mere background, we are not conscious of their meaning because the heart, the core of ourselves, is caught up in God.

I am not quite sure what to think of Abbot Chapman's test. But that the *ligature* occurs, and that it marks the entry into contemplative prayer, is quite certain. Abbot Chapman is also quite right when he says that one of the signs that we are called to contemplative prayer is our simple inability to pray in any other way. Once we experience this, we must not conclude that the spirit of prayer has dried up in us, nor that we are going slightly mad, nor that we have already gone completely mad. What we should conclude is that we are being called into wordless contemplation, and our proper response is simply to relax and let the Holy Spirit take over.

Why have I spoken as such length about this form of prayer? First, because it clearly developed quite early in monastic circles and is very much part of the monastic tradition. It has been a continuous practice in Benedictine monasteries of the English Congregation until the present time, going back to the teachings and writings of the seventeenth century monk, Fr Augustine Baker, who is surely one of the greatest writers on prayer that there has ever been, and whose works deserve to be better known. Baker himself, of course, did not invent this teaching but inherited it from earlier centuries while 'fleshing it out' from his own experience. We can therefore say that this sort of prayer is an intrinsic part of the Benedictine Spiritual Way, which is the subject of this book.

My other reason for talking so much about it is that many people outside monasteries are becoming aware of it and taking an interest in it. This is surely a healthy phenomenon. The story of the Curé d'Ars, also the *Spiritual Letters* of Abbot Chapman, support the view that quite ordinary people can be called to pray in this way. Perhaps it is especially needed in the twentieth century. Our culture is overloaded with words; we are bombarded with them, supersaturated with them, through newspapers, magazines, television, radio, advertising, political and commercial propaganda. To listen in silence to the Word beyond all words is becoming a practice which more and more of us actually need; therefore the Holy Spirit gives us the grace to be able to do it.

Do it, then, we should, provided the basic conditions are fulfilled. First, our prayer should be securely grounded on Christ, flowering out of our contact with him through Scriptures and sacraments. Second, it should be the real thing, genuine prayer relating to God, not mere mental vacuity. Third, we have to be called to it, and be ready to carried into it and out of it as the Holy Spirit prompts us.

We should choose a place for it which is as quiet and solitary as possible. Our posture should be neither tense nor sloppy, but a healthy balance between the two. If we are praying through the repetition of a word or phrase, then we will probably find that our breathing becomes deeper and slower. Attempts to deliberately control the pace of breathing are dangerous and bring in too much of the Self; it is better to let the breath find its own natural rhythm. As for how much we should do – as much as we can, without straining or forcing, and without disrupting our lives.

Prayer, both individual and communal, is the centre of our lives. Also important, however, is the question of how we relate to each other and how we pursue our activities in the world. These will be the topics of our last two chapters.

CHAPTER 11

HUMILITY

THE GERMAN PHILOSOPHER Nietsche despised Christianity because it advocates what he considered to be slave virtues – meekness, gentleness and humility. He thought that we should rather seek to imitate the virtues of the warrior – independence, strength of will, self-reliance and courage. His strongly asserted claim for the 'Way of the Warrior' loses some of its force when we learn that he himself was a timorous man, hen-pecked and dominated by his sister. Nevertheless, there is something in what he says which awakes an answering echo in all of us. Life is often very tough, after all. Ought we not then to be proud and self-reliant and determined, rather than humble and meek? Is it perhaps true that Christianity is only for slaves, and that fully developed men and women ought to reject it, directing their idealism elsewhere? Is it not better to be a king than a slave?

Such questions go to the very heart of what it means to be a human being and a Christian. Our whole destiny hangs on what we think it is to be a king or slave, proud or humble. Jesus and St Benedict are utterly at one on this matter. What exactly are they telling us? How seriously can we take it?

> When Pilate had Jesus brought before him, he asked, 'Are you the King of the Jews?' Jesus answered, 'You have said so.' *Cf Matthew 27:11*

We should note here that Jesus says neither yes nor no to the question that Pilate asks. This is because the answer depends on what Pilate, and indeed the chief priests, considers to be kingship. As kingship is normally understood, no, Jesus is not a king in that sense. Yet in a different, far deeper sense, yes, he is; indeed he is the only one ultimately, who has a true right to that title.

For us a king is one who rules the world, who has maximum power and authority. Therefore he will possess to a supreme degree the warrior virtues advocated by Nietsche: sternness, self-reliance, strength of will. We would also like him to be just and merciful, of course, but he does not have to be so. If he is not, then he is a cruel king, a tyrant and despot; nevertheless, he remains genuinely a king, for kingship is not essentially about justice or mercy but about power. If the king has power then he is a true king, whether he rules justly or not.

In this sense, then, kings are those who have most power: political, social and military. They also have vast material resources at their disposal; kingship is greatly restricted by poverty. A poor king is hard to take seriously, the very idea is almost a contradiction in terms. Therefore we might say that in the twentieth century the population of the whole Western world has become 'king-like' to a degree never attained by our ancestors. Our science and technology have modified our environment, harnessed the forces of nature, changed the face of the planet. We are all kings in as much as we share in that triumph and enjoy the fruits of it.

The teaching of Jesus flies straight in the face of all these notions and contradicts them radically. Do you want power? he asks. Then you must renounce power. Do you want to rule the world? Then you must renounce the world. Do you want to possess it all? Then you must renounce it all. This is because possessing things enslaves us to them, and slaves cannot be rulers. A millionaire is enslaved by his wealth for it dominates his mind and heart and gives him no rest. Great politicians, too, may seem to have a very high degree of power since their decisions affect the lives of millions. In fact they are tools in the hands of forces much greater than themselves. The historical and prophetic books of the Old Testament delight in making fun of the great rulers of the world and their imaginary power, showing that they are blind instruments in the hands of Providence, who raises them up and puts them down as he chooses. This is not just a fanciful picture. Anyone, even today, in a position of great authority soon finds out that such authority does not by any means carry with it unlimited scope for decision-making. Decisions are continually dominated and conditioned by political, social and economic forces that no-one is in control of. Rulers are only rulers in the sense of being in the 'hot seat'; but their decisions are largely forced upon them and are often hardly their own at all. Furthermore the career of a great political leader is a notoriously fragile and precarious thing. Both rise and fall can be conspicuously dramatic. The Old Testament picture, of kings raised up by God only to be put down again when they have served their purpose, is not so very inapplicable to the modern world after all.

Yet, having said all this, it would be highly inappropriate for any of us to adopt a smug, self-righteous tone about the 'power mania' and illusory aims of our political leaders, as though these people were greatly different from us and as though we were ourselves untouched by the malady which affects them. The desire for power, wealth and authority is present to some degree in us all, and nothing is gained by failing to acknowledge the fact. Like all human drives the desire for power is raw, natural, psychic energy, and as such has nothing evil about it, provided it is properly channelled and redirected to less illusory ends. The teaching of Jesus, and of St Benedict after him, are devoted to showing us how to do this, not only by words but also by deeds. In the Sermon on the Mount Jesus taught us how to be kings and to renounce power; he then endured the cross and triumphed over it to show us what kingship means in practice. St Benedict, too, not only wrote the Rule, but lived it out himself, as St Gregory the Great tells us; and the essentially practical nature of this teaching has been proved by generations of monks since.

Humility is the key-virtue, certainly for monks but also for all Christians. It is the essence of the Sermon on the Mount. It is the subject of the longest chapter in St Benedict's Rule. What, then, is it all about? Is it really a servile, cringing sort of virtue, inconsistent with human dignity? Or does it express the truth about what we are, and about how to relate to each other and to God?

Most of us can see, at any rate on the intellectual level, that it expresses the truth about where we stand in relation to God. God is infinite, all-wise, all-good, all-powerful, and we are none of these things. In comparison with him we are nothing at all. We are utterly dependent upon him for everything: our existence, our life, and the very fact that we have a world to exist and live in. None of this is our own, inalienable property, we have no 'right' to any of it. It can all be taken from us at a moment's notice. Truly God is all and we are nothing. The moment we reflect on this we see that it is so. That does not mean, however, that we <u>feel</u> it to be so; still less that we <u>act</u> as though it were so. The anonymous writer of the

157

Cloud of Unknowing draws a sharp distinction between knowing that we are nothing – almost any of us can attain that – and feeling that we are nothing. This last comes only through grace conferred by God upon those who pray deeply. It is a mark of true spiritual progress. The rest of us are not like that. Although we are ready enough to admit our nothingness on the theoretical level, on the level of feeling and practice we live as though we were something. Therefore we are not humble; and because we are not humble we are living in a dream-world; we are not seeing things as they really are. Humility is not a kind of pious charade; it expresses where we really stand in relation to God.

But does it express the truth about where we stand in relation to other people? Most of us would be reluctant to admit this even on the purely theoretical level. St Benedict says that if we are humble then we shall consider all people to be better than ourselves. How can that possibly be true? If a monastery is filled with monks, each one of whom thinks himself worse than everyone else, then someone in that monastery is wrong. Everyone cannot be worse than everyone. It is a logical absurdity. Therefore humility, it seems, does not express the truth about where we stand in relation to each other. It is just a pious pretence, an edifying sort of play-acting.

St Thomas Aquinas, with his usual penetration, saw straight to the heart of this problem and its solution. As a true Dominican, nurtured upon Aristotle, he recognised that virtue is not virtue unless it is founded upon truth. Therefore humility, if it is a genuine virtue, must express the truth, not only about where we stand with God but also about where we stand with each other. St Thomas then faced the problem posed by the Rule of St Benedict which tells us that each one must recognise that he is inferior to everyone else. This, as it stands, is indeed a logical absurdity – unless we recognise that we are expected to look at other people from a standpoint different from that which we adopt when we look at ourselves. When we look at ourselves we should see that which is truly ours, truly our own: sin, imperfection and ultimate nothingness. When we look at others we should strive to see that in them which is from God; for all that is good in them is from God, reflecting his goodness and his glory. We are not comparing the goodness in ourselves with the goodness in other people. We are comparing the nothingness in ourselves – which is our own – with the goodness in other people, which is God's. From this point of view it is perfectly correct and accurate to say that we are worse than everyone else.

But why adopt such a peculiar perspective? Why cannot we compare the good in ourselves with the good in others, comparing like with like? Because this leads quickly to error and illusion, which in turn lead to pride and the disruption of harmonious social relationships. For us to be able to make an accurate comparison of the good in ourselves and the good in others we would need to have a complete and exact knowledge of ourselves and of others. We have no such knowledge. We do not know ourselves and we do not know others, either. Furthermore, our natural tendency when comparing ourselves with other people is to magnify our own virtues and minimise those of others. Comparisons of this kind are, therefore, not merely odious but also dangerous and misleading. By comparing our own nothingness with the good in others we remain on safe ground, within the limit of what we genuinely know. It also trains us to develop a more

159

positive attitude towards other people than we normally have. It trains us to look for the good qualities of other people instead of pouncing on their defects. Looking for these good qualities leads us to find them; we always find what we look for, and indeed these good qualities are always there to be found. It is remarkable how often doing this enables us to establish, or re-establish, relations with a person whom we previously found impossible. Once we see that person's good side we can then use that as a bridge, or as a foundation, on which to build a relationship.

There still remains a problem, however. What of the good qualities which we really possess, and know that we possess? Does humility require that we try to fool ourselves and pretend that we do not have them? Here again we are moving into the idea that humility is pretence rather than truth, since it does not rest upon facts. Many people, indeed, do see humility in this way; as CS Lewis says somewhere, we think it means a beautiful woman pretending she is ugly or an intelligent one pretending she is stupid. But in fact we are not required by humility to fool ourselves like this. We may know that we have good qualities, but we should not advert to them when comparing ourselves with other people. Similarly we may know that other people have faults but we should not advert to them when comparing them with ourselves. In this way we shall avoid the distortions and errors of perspective which come about whenever we look at ourselves and others in our normal, natural way.

There may be times, of course, when we can safely recognise the good qualities and gifts we have, because we are not using them as a basis for comparison with other people. If I am made monastic choirmaster, for example, I may be thankful that God has given me a musical gift which enables me to do the job. If, however, I then start to feel superior to those who have no such gift, then I am in trouble, for I am comparing myself with others; and it is a very odious comparison. If I think myself to be the best choirmaster the monastery has ever had, then I am in very serious trouble indeed. God does, indeed, give us qualities and gifts, but these are not meant to be feathers to be made into a head-dress; they are tools to be used for the glory of God and the good of others. They are free gifts from God; we did not give them to ourselves, so we can take no credit for them. They are given to us, further-more, for service, not for self-aggrandisement. We can never do enough for God, nor for other people. Whatever gifts we have, therefore, and however vigorously we use them, we have to say finally that we are unworthy servants. This is humility. It is also realism. It expresses the truth about our relationship to God and to others.

This is all clearly recognised by St Benedict in his policy concerning monks who have a gift for craft-work. Let them, he says, practise their craft and, if they can, earn money by it for the community. But if they grow vain and conceited about what they are doing they should be taken off it until their pride has been deflated and they come to a more realistic assessment of themselves and their contribution to the com-munity's life. This principle is valid for everyone, whatever their gift may be, whether it be for preaching, or writing, or spiritual direction, or administration, or finance. We accept the gift gratefully from God, and use it not for ourselves but for others.

The sober realism of all this, and the unselfish generosity which it implies, shows us that there is nothing servile or cringing about humility, nothing that violates the truth about what we are. It is a very high virtue indeed and makes the warrior virtues admired by Nietsche look extremely fatuous and inflated, as indeed they are. To maintain the perspective of humility throughout life is not at all easy. It calls for a very high measure of self-discipline, quite as rigorous as anything which might form part of a warrior's training. Indeed it is impossible to attain this virtue by natural means. We have to pray for it. It is a supernatural gift.

In this respect it is clearly distinguishable from modesty. Humility and modesty are not at all the same thing. Modesty means simply not making a display of our good qualities or gifts, but drawing a discreet veil over them. It is a purely natural virtue, a kind of tact and politeness which can be dictated to us by social convention and simple prudence. But to actually see oneself as nothing before God and before other people – we are well out of the natural domain here. For this we need a special inspiration of the Holy Spirit. We must pray for it, and wait patiently for it to come. Outwardly we try to act in a humble way, while praying for the time to come when it will not be a merely external practice but it will take root firmly in the heart.

We must also recognise that its coming will be gradual. Humility is a virtue which we acquire progressively; if all goes as it should we advance in it from day to day. Therefore St Benedict speaks of steps in humility, comparing them to the rungs of a ladder which we climb one by one. We should beware of taking this image too literally. I do not think that St Benedict's list of steps is meant to be chronological, in the sense that having mastered the first step we move on to the next, and so on. That cannot be right, for the third step of humility is said to be 'obedience without delay' and that is required of a monk from the very first day of his entry into the monastery. It is no use his saying to the Abbot: 'Oh no, I can't obey you yet because that's the third step of humility and I'm still working on the first.' The steps are not chronological in that sense; we are meant to work on all of them every day. Neither are they chronological in the sense of describing <u>stages</u> in the spiritual life which unfold successively, like the *Dark Night of the Senses* and the *Dark Night of the Soul* described by St John of the Cross. Attempts have been made to interpret them in this way, but they do not really work. It is better to see them as simply so many different ways in which humility manifests itself in our life and behaviour. As for the image of a ladder with its rungs, this is surely meant simply to suggest the idea of <u>movement</u> and progress in the development of this virtue. This is a true picture, since we continue to work at it and grow in it from day to day until the end of our lives.

Is there any particular logic, then, in the order in which St Benedict lists these rungs or steps? Certainly there is an element of the arbitrary in both the order and the number. St Benedict's list of twelve steps is based upon an earlier one by St John Cassian, who lists only ten steps, which furthermore do not correspond exactly to St Benedict's. Also St Benedict seems to have changed his mind about the order. In the chapter on Obedience, for example, he says, 'The first step of humility is unhesitating obedience' which contradicts what he says in the chapter on Humility, where the first step of humility is said to be the 'fear of God.' This suggests that he started out with a notion of order and number which he subsequently changed. Yet the order given in the chapter on

THE PATH OF LIFE

Humility seems to represent his final view, and there is a certain logic in it. The first step, the 'fear of God' is fundamental in that it expresses the basic <u>attitude</u> of mind and heart which is the essence of the virtue: the sense of our own nothingness before God and before other people. The other steps, describing restraint in speech, manner and general behaviour, can therefore be seen as various different ways in which this fundamental attitude manifests itself in our daily life. They are variations upon the one basic theme. The first step, then, is first because it is basic and primary; but from then on the order of the steps is fairly arbitrary. Certainly I have never been convinced by any attempt to find meaning in it.

One thing, however, is beyond all reasonable doubt, and that is that St Benedict clearly sees humility as the key virtue, the ground or basis of every other. That may surprise us, for we are used to thinking that the Christian spiritual path is all about love. So it is, but love is not genuine unless it is based upon humility. Humility is the root; love is the flower. We cannot love God properly unless we see where we really stand in relation to him; we cannot love other people properly unless we see where we really stand in relation to them. Love which is not grounded upon humility turns quickly into illusion, possessiveness and desire. There has to be an element of awe, of reverent fear, governing our relationships, whether with God or with other people. We have sentimentalised our idea of love, so that we no longer see that fear or reverent awe are part of it. We are too casually familiar with God, treating him as a 'buddy' or 'chum'; to talk, as St Benedict does, about the 'fear of God' has become very unfashionable. We are too casual and loose and sentimental, also, about our relationships with other people. This comes out in practically

164

all our modern translations of the Rule, which render St Benedict as saying that the Abbot should strive to be 'loved rather than feared' – suggesting that the Abbot should not be feared at all. That is not, however, what St Benedict actually says. He does not say 'loved rather than feared' – in Latin *potius quam* – but 'loved more than feared' – in Latin *magis quam*. In other words, love is meant to be predominate in our relationships with the Abbot, yet there is an element also of fear. Not fear in the sense that we fear a hurricane or a poisonous snake; rather, fear in the sense of reverent awe. This should be the foundation of our attitude, both to God in prayer, and to other people in our daily life with them. Only if we are humble can we truly love.

We have talked a lot here about humility as a fundamental attitude of mind. That is its intrinsic nature or essence. But what about the various concrete ways in which we are meant to realise it in practise? What about the other rungs in St Benedict's ladder?

In general these are aimed at teaching us moderation, restraint and self-effacement, in our speech, deportment and general behaviour. They are meant to discourage us from being splashy, self-assertive or manipulative. We concentrate on showing respect for other people, their views and needs, rather than our own. It is in this sense that we should understand St Benedict's steps and apply them to our own situation in the modern world. This calls for a certain measure of finesse and adaptability, for there is a certain culture gap between St Benedict's world and ours, so that some of his precepts, if taken literally, would produce the opposite effect from that intended. Always to walk, for example, with one's head bowed while brooding on one's sins would for us, in our culture, quickly become a sort of 'ham' acting, which would lead to an unhealthy preoccupation with ourselves. Such preoccupation is a straight denial of humility, which is aimed rather at a simple, natural self-forgetfulness. If I brood incessantly upon my own sins, then I cannot forget this 'I' and never become truly humble. Cardinal Basil Hume, when he was Abbot of Ampleforth, often used to tell his monks, 'Take God seriously; take other people seriously; but never, never take yourself seriously.' That is a very skilful translation of St Benedict's basic idea into the terms of our modern culture.

Some of the greatest spiritual teachers of the past have considered that, in order to be truly humble, we should actively seek out humiliating circumstances and experiences. St John of the Cross, for example, says that we should always speak ill of ourselves and try to get others to speak ill of us, too. One hesitates to question the precepts of so great a saint; yet there is something here of the fierce and ascetic piety of sixteenth-century Spain which does not transmit well into the twentieth-century. Here again, if we today were to affirm our lowliness in this fierce way, this could quickly become a subtle form of self-assertion. 'I am nothing. I am a worm. I am useless at everything. I am hopelessly inferior to everyone else.' There is too much 'I' here for genuine humility to dawn.

If humiliating experiences come to us unsought, however, then we should accept them and 'bow beneath the mighty hand of God.' We may fail in our ideals, and commit serious sins. In that case we should acknowledge our weakness and infidelity, not dressing it up or hiding it, but admitting it frankly and casting ourselves upon God's mercy. This can be done even in small matters. A novice, for example, should not say, 'I was washing a cruet and it slipped form between my fingers and it broke.' He should rather say, quite simply, 'I have broken a cruet.' We cannot live for very long with other people without, sooner or later, being forced to recognise our own weaknesses and imperfections. Indeed, any community, whether in a monastery or in a family out in the world, always contains a certain number of people who feel they have a certain gift of the Holy Spirit for pointing out our faults. Yet we should not rebel against this but recognise the truth in what is said. Humility is, furthermore, an essential basis for obedience. It is hard to obey when the superior orders us to do something which seems absurd or wrong. Humility helps us to obey by reminding us that we do not always know what is best for us. We ought to at least consider the possibility that the superior may be right.

Humility is true; it does not deny the fact of who and what we are. Humility also calls for great control and self-discipline, since it contradicts so many natural tendencies. It calls, furthermore, for great energy and dedication in our service to God and to other people. Although we do not take to ourselves the credit for what we do, we are expected to use all our powers of thought, feeling and action in the service that we render, thus realising our full potential as human beings. Perhaps, then, Jesus and St Benedict were right and Nietsche was wrong. A full human life is one in which we have the right relationship with God and with each other. That is guaranteed only by humility. It should govern our prayer and our very activity. It is, indeed, the key virtue.

CHAPTER 12

MAKING LIFE A UNITY

L ABORARE EST ORARE − to work is to pray. This saying has been handed down over the centuries and is usually attributed to St Benedict. In fact, there is no evidence whatever that he actually said it. I do not believe that he could have said it. It does not represent his mind; and furthermore it is not true. Certainly work can be prayer; but that depends upon the attitude and frame of mind with which we approach it. A great deal of St Benedict's teaching is devoted to showing us how to develop and apply this frame of mind.

We are touching now upon a very fundamental and important problem, which is: how to make the whole of our life holy. What we normally do is to divide our life into separate, watertight compartments. On the one hand there is the 'religious' compartment (if we are religious at all) − communal and private prayer, spiritual reading, and perhaps a few activities done for the local church. On the other hand there is the 'worldly' compartment (though we may not call it that). This includes our work, our personal relationships, and the various experiences we undergo from day to day. The tendency is for us to keep these compartments absolutely separate. There is no overflow from one into the other. There are even people who think that there should not be any such overflow, that it is something to be prevented at all costs. Perhaps most human beings incline to this view from time to time; but it is particularly common among the English. One of the most deeply-rooted convictions in the minds of many English people is that 'religion' must be kept strictly separate from 'life'. This idea that religion might overflow and affect all areas of life is felt to be profoundly shocking, and even rather immoral. Some years ago I met a man who disapproved strongly of the Roman Catholic Church for this precise reason: that it calls its members to a total commitment involving all areas of life. In other words, the Roman Catholic Church commits the unpardonable sin of 'not knowing its place.' It is very important that religion should know its place and keep out of territory where it has no business.

Jesus of Nazareth most emphatically did not allow his religion to know its place. His devotion to his Father and to his Father's work engulfed his life totally. He expected the same commitment from his followers. So did St Benedict. For both of these men the distinction between the religious and the worldly is impossible, because for them the worldly simply does not exist. It should not exist for any of us, either. If it comes into existence in our life then that is the result of sin, or imperfection, or weakness. It is a wound to be healed, a malady to be cured as quickly as possible. We have to act very promptly and resolutely, because if we do not then the malady spreads. The result of dividing life into religious and worldly is that the worldly dimension grows and grows until the religious dimension is eclipsed and finally disappears altogether. That is something which has already happened on a large scale in the modern western world. Many ills have resulted from this, and continue to do so.

To heal this rift, however, to bridge this gap, is by no means an easy business. It is made harder by the fact that very little guidance is available on how to do it. In any religious bookshop we shall find an enormous number of slim paperbacks telling us how to pray or meditate; there are plenty of books, too, telling us how to conduct our personal relationships, our moral and social lives; and we undergo training for our work, whatever it may be. But no-one tells us how to pull these various strands together to make a single piece of cloth, a seamless garment. No-one tells us how to bring the various clashing elements into some sort of harmony or unity.

So am I going to leap in with both feet and attempt what no-one else has attempted? It is with some degree of trepidation that I contemplate the prospect. If I do attempt it, then it must be clearly understood that I am not talking from the standpoint of one who has 'solved it all' and can therefore solve it for others as well. I speak as one who still has everything to learn, who struggles with the problem anew every day. Yet within the framework of Benedictine life there are certain guidelines and certain resources to draw on. These have saved me on many occasions, if not from all disaster then at least from total disaster. Therefore it might be worth trying to share them with those who might profit from them.

Let no-one imagine that monks are in some way immune to the problem of compartmentalisation. Most communities today work very hard, using modern means and methods. This puts them under the same pressures as those which affect people outside the monastic environment. We are all part of the late twentieth century world: there are the same problems, the same challenges, the same opportunities for us all. This is, of course, a certain religious structure to a monks life, pointing in a spiritual direction. This structure, however, has to be used, and it not always is. The gospel says that to those who have, more shall be given; but those who have not shall lose even what they think they have. Benedictine monks have many resources to draw on, but if full use is not made of them, then the monk is no better off than people in the world. He may even end up worse off. People in the world who establish a firm spiritual foundation to their lives, and learn to live their whole lives on that basis, are in a better situation than some monks. This present chapter aims at giving a few hints and suggestions on how this foundation might be laid and built upon. It summarises and develops what has been said in previous chapters.

Let us assume, then, that we are praying every day, as much as we can manage. Let us assume that we resort frequently to the sacraments. Let us assume that we do at least some lectio or spiritual reading each day, even if it is no more than a few lines of Scripture. Let us assume that we have at least some notion of what St Benedict means by listening, and of the substance of the three vows, and that we want to realise these ideals in our lives. How do we integrate into this all the other elements which our lives are composed of, elements which often seem resistant, if not actually hostile, to any spiritual aim?

St Benedict saw humility as the key virtue, the only secure foundation for any spiritual life. So it is. It is also the key to solving this problem, of how to bring all the disparate elements of our life and experience into some sort of unity.

First of all, humility must be the foundation of all our prayer. Everything that St Benedict says about prayer either states or implies this; yet it is a truth which is not always understood. We do not pray from a standpoint of strength but of weakness. If we rely only on our own natural resources we cannot actually pray at all. Prayer is only true and effective when the Holy Spirit takes over, praying in us and through us, whether

171

we are praying the Eucharist, the Liturgy of the Hours, or our own private prayer. Prayer, then, whatever form it takes, is first and foremost this act of <u>surrender</u> to the Holy Spirit, without whom nothing can happen at all. This is humility in prayer, whereby we recognise that God is everything and we are nothing. The more we efface ourselves before him, the more we cast everything upon him (including our boredom and distraction), the deeper and more valid our prayer will be. It is from this attitude of humility that our love for God will grow and flower. We only really begin to love God genuinely when we realise our total dependence upon him, his compassion and his mercy. As we sink deeply into our own darkness and nothingness we find, mysteriously, that a light shines forth out of the heart of it. There can be no light, however, without a previous darkness, which is entered through humility.

Now we come to the difficult bit, which spiritual books do not normally talk about. This humble, reverent attitude of awe and surrender has to be maintained also outside prayer, in the normal activities and experiences of our daily life. In a way, this is extremely hard, yet in another way it is remarkably simple and easy.

It is best to start in small ways. There is a practice which I have found very useful, especially on those occasions when life does not seem to be going too well – prayer is difficult and dry, human relationships hard to maintain, work oppressive and unrewarding. I go into a quiet room and sit there for a while on my own, not doing anything, not even praying, but simply being relaxed, docile, and attentive. I become aware of various things – the slant of the sun's rays as they fall upon the floor or upon the table; the sound of the wind in the trees outside, or a passing car. I feel the pressure of my body upon the chair, the rhythm of my breathing and of my heartbeat. Thoughts flow in a random fashion, and I let them do so, without interfering with them, but also without letting myself dwell on any of them. I simply remain relaxed and attentive, aware of all the elements in the present situation and <u>remaining</u> within that situation, not letting my mind wander into the past or the future.

People who do this may well find that the mind gradually settles and grows calm as they become increasingly aware of themselves and of their surroundings, simply settling into the situation without interfering with it or in any way seeking to change it. Some have spoken of a Presence which becomes perceptible as the various elements of the situation align themselves around a Centre, like iron filings around a magnet – the Centre being invisible, imperceptible, and even, in a sense, empty, although it is the source of all life and meaning. At such times the mind often moves naturally into prayer, very simple and quiet. This comes from having accepted a perfectly ordinary, everyday, basic situation in a humble, docile, and receptive way. That situation thus becomes an icon, a reflection of God, a place of encounter.

Having done this in silence and solitude we can then move on to try it in situations where there is more movement and activity; for example, while walking down the street on the way to work. Again, we try to be relaxed and aware, open to everything which we perceive, but not fixing the mind on anything in particular. Buses passing, lights in shop windows, the faces of people hurrying by, the various sights and sounds streaming through the senses – we simply take all this in, not resisting any of it, not holding on to any of it. The more we do this the more the clashing elements of the situation are resolved and harmonised into a unity which we cannot express in words but nevertheless we sense to be there. Again, an ordinary, everyday situation is becoming an icon and a place of encounter with God, through our having approached it with humility and reverence.

It is much harder to do this in our relationships with other people – at any rate, for me it is quite hard, though others may well be better at it. We are not usually humble or self-effacing in our relationships with others. Rather our tendency is to be selfish and manipulative. We try to charm some, while freezing others off; sometimes we try to glitter and dazzle and show off, while at other times we are glum and uncommunicative. All of this comes from seeing others merely from the standpoint of self – how they relate to me, to my needs, to my hopes, fears, and wishes. This is pride, for I am thus behaving as though I were the centre of the universe, and other people's lives, personalities, and activities have meaning only in relation to me. The fatuous absurdity of this becomes apparent the moment we advert to it. Usually, however, we do not advert to it. It takes perseverance, practice, and the grace of God to recognise that other people have value in themselves, for what they are and what there is of God in them, quite independently of me, of my aims and wishes.

There is a subtle spiritual art which consists of being quite empty and colourless in oneself, like a piece of glass whose transparency allows the light to shine through it unimpeded. Other people's words, deeds, and personalities stream into us while we remain simply open and receptive, accepting without judging. This is humility, for it is effacing oneself before the mystery of others. However, there is an important

174

difference here, which distinguishes this sort of situation from those more private ones described earlier; for here we have to make a some sort of response to these people whom we are encountering. We have to take a more active, rather than a merely passive, rôle. Yet humility can come in here as well, for all depends upon the nature of the responses we make and the initiatives we take with other people Are we going to manipulate them, bend them to our own will? Or are we going to encourage them to be themselves, to draw them out, to help them express what they truly are?

I once met a lady who was brilliant at this. In company she never tried to glitter, never tried to charm or repel people. She merely drew out what was in them. People talking to her found that they were expressing wise thoughts, or dazzling witticisms, which they would not normally have thought themselves capable of. They often congratulated themselves secretly on their remarkable performance, thinking that it was all due to themselves. It was not. It was mainly due to her. She had the art of drawing people out. And, who knows, perhaps God would occasionally allow her to meet her match, someone who would draw her out, help her to express what was deep inside her.

I have sometimes thought that we ought to approach other people rather like a skilful landscape gardener, who does not try to impose his own notions of order upon nature, but rather looks for the order already implicit in it, then, gently and delicately, helps this order to emerge more clearly. Therefore, instead of producing something like the monstrous and absurd formal gardens of the eighteenth century, where natural features are obliterated and trees and shrubs trained into bizarre and unnatural geometrical shapes, a truly skilful gardener would expend far less effort, but would simply round off a feature here, trim a little there, not imposing his own meaning but simply drawing the landscape out, helping it to articulate its own inherent meaning.

We are aggressive and domineering with nature, as we are with each other, so the image of God is obliterated and we live in a hellish world, and society is simply the creation of our own diseased minds and wills. A little more humility might do much to mend this, so that the presence of God would become more perceptible, both in our world and in our society.

St Benedict says that we should pray before undertaking any good work. It is not at all a bad idea for us to pray, very briefly and sincerely, when in company and in conversation with others. This is particularly useful in situations of tension, when the atmosphere is electric with fear, anger, or hostility. Simply relax, open the eyes, ears, and heart, and settle into the situation, feeling intuitively for its centre. Pray briefly and secretly to Christ, asking him to come and dwell at the heart of it. Then, do or say whatever seems necessary, whatever the Spirit prompts. This is all a form of listening, for we are seeking to be aware of other people as they really are, rather than what we would like them to be. It is also a form of humility, since we do not behave towards them as we feel like behaving, but simply do or say what the situation actually requires. This we cannot know unless we let go of our own ideas and wants, opening ourselves up docilely and receptively to others and their needs.

Such humility does not mean that there are no occasions when we have to be energetic and even rather stern. How could that be so? Moses, when he saw that a golden calf had been made, had it ground down and the dust scattered on the water and made the Hebrews drink it. That is quite stern action, yet we are told that 'the man Moses was very meek, the meekest upon the face of the earth.' (*Numbers 12:3*) Similarly, the humility of Jesus is beyond question, yet he shouted at Peter, saying, 'Get behind me, Satan!' and drove the moneychangers out of the Temple by physical force. St Benedict, also, does not expect the abbot to be soft, but ready to reprove and correct when necessary. Yet the abbot is also warned that he will be held to account to God for his treatment of the brethren. Sternness must not be motivated by caprice, or by ordinary human anger, bad temper, or pique. It must be inspired by God, by zeal for justice, and by real concern for the people involved. This needs to be borne in mind by anyone who has authority over others – not only abbots, but parents, employers, and superiors as well. We are trying to develop a sense of how to treat people which is based upon their needs and upon the will of God, not our own moods and desires. Here again, a brief, secret prayer in the heat of the moment can help us ensure that our words and actions are coming from the right place.

Humility in human relationships involves recognising the mystery in other people, that which we do not know and perhaps can never know. However close we are to a person, there will always be certain things which we cannot know about or share with that person. It is important to recognise this, and not resent it. A husband who grows jealous when he sees his wife sharing something with another man which he cannot share with her himself, is being neither realistic nor humble. He is not giving her space to be herself. For human relationships to grow and to last, we have to give other people this space. We cannot expect to be with them, on top of them, all the time. This is part of that generous self-effacement before others which is a large part of humility and is simply recognising the mystery which is in them. As CS Lewis says, we have to remember that no human being can ever totally fulfil another human being. We have to let our wives, or husbands, or children, be themselves and on occasions have the magnanimity to stand back and let others take over. This is all humility, letting God into the situation. If we are worried about the situation we should remain still and silent, committing it to God, not intervening unless we are fairly sure that this is the right thing to do.

I have sometimes found myself fretting because I have not heard from a certain close friend for some time. Yet how silly this is, and what a lack of trust it shows. My friends have their own lives to live, their own work to do. If they have not had the time, or felt the need, to write or telephone should I therefore conclude that the relationship is crumbling? Patience, trust in God, and the ability to stand back and wait are indispensable in all human relationships. It is selfish pride, not humility, if we expect our friends to be bombarding us continually with signs of affection and concern. Can we not let them be themselves, and let them express what they want when they want? Do we genuinely love them, or do we merely want to dominate them? There have been times when I have been horrified to see myself turning into a sort of pagan idol, who expects to be kept happy all the time by offerings and incense. I am not alone in this tendency.

Finally, something needs to be said about work. We all have to work, and some of us have work which is not very rewarding or fulfilling. It is not easy to integrate this into the spiritual life. Problems arise, too, when we do enjoy our work, for then it can become a form of self-assertion which undermines humility and drives out God.

The spiritual key to all work is the <u>motive</u> from which it is done. That is the reason why, in my own Benedictine community, novices are given only very ordinary, humdrum work, which is not at all exciting or rewarding. Since they cannot find meaning or fulfilment in the work itself, they are therefore obliged to find it in the motive underlying it. If what we do is for the glory of God and the good of others, and we remember this continually, then it ceases to be a meaningless chore. It really does, in this case, become a form of prayer.

We can, of course, sometimes do actual prayer during it. If it is boring, repetitive work which does not demand full attention – like shelling peas, peeling potatoes, or washing up – we can let the mind rest in God while doing it, perhaps with the occasional brief invocation. Most of us have a certain amount of this sort of thing to do each day. It loses much of its oppressiveness and tedium once we treat it like the other situations described earlier in this chapter. settling into it and feeling intuitively for its spiritual centre.

What of that work which demands our full attention, so that we cannot pray during it? We can, at any rate, do what St Benedict says, and pray before it and after it, offering it all to God. However demanding it is there will be moments, too, when we pause to take breath or relax. Why not relax in God? Why not rest in God? Meister Eckhart once said that when we are tired and the day is long, we should rest in God, in whom there is no fatigue and no time. That is echoing the words of Jesus in St John's Gospel, saying, 'The Father, who is the source of life, has made the Son the source of life.'

To remain relaxed and calm while energetically working, to be at rest in the midst of action, is a great spiritual art. Time, practice, perseverance, and the grace of God are all needed in order to acquire it. To maintain the same attitude in situations of pain, dereliction and loss, is even harder. Yet it is possible. Jesus gave us an example of it in the cross, surrendering and submitting to the worst of all possible experiences, in the words: 'Father, into your hands I commend my spirit.'

It should be clear from what has been said in this book that the spiritual path of the monk is not fundamentally different from that of the ordinary Christian. In both cases the aim is the same: to ground the whole of our life and experience upon God. The monk is helped in this by having certain resources at his disposal. Many of these can be participated in by non-monks, though not to the same extent. They are more fully and continually available to the monk, and that is probably why some people are called to be monks – they need to have these resources fully available and could not survive spiritually without them. Others who are not monks can, nevertheless, share in them to some degree, as I hope this book has shown. If used continually from day to day they will give shape, meaning, and direction to our life. We shall grow steadily in our relationship with God and with each other. We shall learn to surrender to the magnetic pull of God in all circumstances. It will not always be easy or comfortable. Sometimes we shall be carried into turbulent waters and dark tunnels. Nevertheless, if we hold onto trust in God, we shall emerge safely from all these difficulties and adversities. We shall fulfil the purpose for which we were created. This is truly 'the path of life' of which the Psalmist speaks. Even in this present world we shall experience some of the reward which comes from following this path. The rest lies beyond the grave; we wait for and look forward to it in patience and in hope.